27

-7 JAN 2010
WITHDRAWN
EAST SUSSEX COUNTY COUNCIL

D0585942

THE
LEADER'S WAY

THE
LEADER'S WAY

BUSINESS, BUDDHISM AND HAPPINESS IN AN INTERCONNECTED WORLD

HIS HOLINESS THE DALAI LAMA

& LAURENS VAN DEN MUYZENBERG

NICHOLAS BREALEY
PUBLISHING

LONDON · BOSTON

First published
in Great Britain
by Nicholas Brealey Publishing in 2008

3–5 Spafield Street
Clerkenwell, London
EC1R 4QB, UK
Tel: +44 (0)20 7239 0360
Fax: +44 (0)20 7239 0370
www.nicholasbrealey.com
www.leadersway.org

© His Holiness the Dalai Lama and Laurens van den Muyzenberg, 2008
The rights of His Holiness the Dalai Lama and Laurens van den
Muyzenberg to be identified as the authors of this work have been
asserted in accordance with the Copyright, Designs and Patents Act 1988.

ISBN: 978-1-85788-511-8

British Library Cataloguing in Publication Data
A catalogue record for this book is available from the British Library.

All rights reserved. No part of this publication may be reproduced, stored
in a retrieval system, or transmitted, in any form or by any means,
electronic, mechanical, photocopying, recording and/or otherwise
without the prior written permission of the publishers. This book may
not be lent, resold, hired out or otherwise disposed of by way of trade in
any form, binding or cover other than that in which it is published,
without the prior consent of the publishers.

FSC

Printed in Finland by WS Bookwell
on Forest Stewardship Council certified paper.

CONTENTS

Introduction   1
The Monk and the Management Consultant   7

PART I: LEADING YOURSELF   **11**

Chapter One: Taking the Right View   13
Chapter Two: Doing the Right Thing   29
Chapter Three: Training Your Mind   47

PART II: LEADING YOUR ORGANIZATION   **67**

Chapter Four: The Leader's Purpose   69
Chapter Five: Creating Profit, Jobs – or Happiness?   91
Chapter Six: Doing Business Right   111

**PART III: LEADING IN AN
INTERCONNECTED WORLD**   **131**

Chapter Seven: The Challenge of Globalization   133
Chapter Eight: Entrepreneurship and Poverty   149
Chapter Nine: The Responsible Free-Market Economy   171

Epilogue   185
Notes   187
Index   193
Acknowledgments   201

EAST SUSSEX COUNTY LIBRARY	
03444854	
Macaulay	Inv 145520
658.4092	£ 16.99
30 Oct 08	EAS. 11/08

INTRODUCTION

His Holiness the Dalai Lama

G ENERALLY BUDDHIST MONKS are somewhat isolated from the rest of society, often secluded in peace while praying for the welfare of all sentient beings and for our planet. Although I am one such monk, I also have responsibilities with regard to the Tibetan government-in-exile, which offers me a broader perspective in that I interact with people from all over the world. In the course of my travels I have met many different kinds of people, some of them poor, some of them rich, each of them occupying their own position in the world. People appear to trust me and therefore many have talked to me about their lives, and their hopes and concerns about the future. This is how I have learned a great deal about what people are looking for. In the end, what almost everyone is seeking is a measure of happiness.

Why am I writing this book now? Because I feel we all should have a sincere concern and take responsibility for how the global economy operates, and an interest in the role of businesses in shaping our interconnectedness. Times have changed and I believe that leaders of religious traditions – with their ability to take a long view – should participate in discussions of global business and economics. Our world faces very serious problems. Those that are of particular concern to me include how to alleviate poverty in poor countries; the fact that even in prosperous countries the sense of satisfaction with life has been stagnating since 1950; the negative impact on the environment

1

that is a result of negligence and of our ever-increasing population and rising standard of living; and finally, the lack of peace in many parts of the world.

Because Buddhism takes a rational and logical attitude to such problems, its approach is sometimes easier to understand for those who are not religious. There is a stress on human values and on how we can be taught to take a holistic approach to solving society's problems. This is an important contribution that Buddhism can make to these discussions. If we view Buddhist teachings in terms of secular ethics and fundamental human values, then perhaps they too have something to contribute to the business world. Buddhist concepts about wealth, work, consumption, and happiness are somewhat different than their Western counterparts. Happiness is different than merely satisfying our material and other wishes; this distinction is important. The root of happiness is not in what we desire or what we get but somewhere altogether different. It stems from a place of contentment that exists no matter what we gain or achieve.

Buddha recognized that self-oriented drives were very powerful. However, he came to the conclusion that the drive for satisfying the desires of the self was impossible to achieve, a never-ending cycle. People cannot be truly happy unless they have friendships and good relationships with other people. Furthermore, good relationships are reciprocal. It is impossible for people to build positive relationships with others if their only aim is to satisfy their own desires. I believe that governments and organizations enter the equation because they bring people into contact with one another; they create jobs and wealth, and they have a very important role to play in these questions of the standard of living and human happiness – and where the two may intersect.

I do not pretend that the solutions we need are simple or straightforward. While working on this book, I have come to understand how difficult it can be for businesspeople to make the right decisions. When the leader of a company makes a decision, it affects all the employees and many others who buy its products or act as suppliers. This becomes especially complex for large, global corporations operating in many countries, and therefore the quality of business decisions is critical. For this reason, the decision maker must not only be competent, but must also have the right motivation and the right state of mind. Competence specific to business measures both talent and knowledge; as such, it is beyond the scope of this book. However, observing and correcting your motivation is an important aspect of Buddhist practice and is discussed in detail here, as is cultivating the right state of mind.

Fundamental to Buddhist philosophy is the notion that suffering exists, and that the Buddha calls on all of us to help alleviate it. My aim is the same: to reduce suffering and increase satisfaction with life as a whole. The purpose of this book is therefore to enable readers and leaders to understand more clearly what happens in their minds and the mind of others, particularly in the context of leadership. As a consequence, I hope you will be able to make different decisions that will generate a better quality of life for yourself, the organizations to which you belong, and everyone else affected by those decisions.

My own interest and thinking about business and economics have evolved over the last 50 years. My formal training has been of an entirely religious and spiritual character. From my youth up until now my field of study has been Buddhist philosophy and psychology. To some extent, due to my interaction with Tibetan and Chinese members of the

Communist Party, I gradually learned about different economic systems. By inclination I found I leaned toward socialism, but I watched as the economies in socialist countries stagnated while the free-market economies grew clearly more dynamic. I became particularly interested in what had gone wrong with the socialist economies and in the positive aspects of the free market. However, I remain concerned that the free-market system tends to increase the gap between the rich and the poor.

In 1990, I received a letter from Laurens van den Muyzenberg, an international management consultant. He suggested that rather than seeking to combine the common themes of communism and Buddhist thinking, as I had earlier envisaged, it would be more effective to consider how capitalism could be improved in an attempt to address our collective concerns. I found the idea appealing and asked him to visit me; we met many times over the intervening years. Then in 1999, Laurens suggested that given the increasing interest in governance among global companies – and the fact that the Buddhist tradition includes many theoretical and practical instructions that would be helpful to people in businesses, especially their leaders – I should be able to make a contribution to the literature on the subject. We agreed at the outset that we wanted this book to be of practical use and to help businesspeople make better decisions. We decided that Laurens would describe the general business background and I would present the application of Buddhist teachings to the issues raised.

I advised Laurens to take a holistic approach. By "holistic" I meant that he should look at issues from many different perspectives, not solely that of a management consultant from the West. I believe one of the main problems in the world today is that, while the amount of information is growing exponentially, people are becoming more and more specialized and are no longer able to understand how all these ideas for improving society interact.

In writing this book I have selected subjects that I think are important and Laurens has investigated them according to his own experience, engaging in discussion with professional colleagues and researching published information. He also interviewed business leaders who were active Buddhist practitioners about the impact of Buddhism on their approach to business. Despite our efforts, we do not claim to have found all the answers. Throughout, we have taken pains to present Buddhist teachings in a way that businesspeople can easily understand.

I am not interested in creating more Buddhists. My interest is to present Buddhist concepts that are acceptable and useful to people from all religious faiths, and to those without any religious faith.

I lost my freedom at the age of 16 and became a refugee at 24. I have faced a great many difficulties in my life. Nevertheless, I have maintained my peace of mind. I can even say that due to my Buddhist training I am happier than many people who take freedom and a country they call their own for granted. This ability to maintain my peace of mind is entirely due to the teachings I have received and my consistent attempt to put them into practice by training my mind. My sincere hope is that this type of training, which is discussed and taught in this book, can be acquired by our leaders – in business and global organizations – to bring about a more peaceful and sustainable planet.

THE MONK AND THE MANAGEMENT CONSULTANT

LAURENS VAN DEN MUYZENBERG

THIS PROJECT IS about the meeting of two worlds: my world of management consulting, more specifically the global marketplace, and the Dalai Lama's world of Tibetan Buddhism. It has been the most exciting and rewarding professional experience of my life.

After I read one of His Holiness's books in which he wrote that an Indian philosopher was working on a synthesis between communism and Buddhism, I wrote to him to say I thought it would be easier to make a synthesis between Buddhism and capitalism. Somewhat to my surprise, I received a letter from His Holiness inviting me to come and visit him in India. From 1991 to 2000 I met with the Dalai Lama every year and did small consulting projects for him, on a voluntary basis, including seminars about strategy for his government in exile.

At the beginning, my knowledge of Buddhist teachings was limited; so too was the Dalai Lama's experience with economics and the world of business. Although His Holiness had studied the socialist system and the works of Karl Marx, his exposure to the free-market system was more limited. The idea was that I would brief the Dalai Lama on an economic area and His Holiness would comment on the issues based on his perspective.

7

These discussions covered many of the basics of business and as such had little to do with Buddhism. However, it soon became clear that the Dalai Lama wanted to understand and see the big picture – how business fits into society and the true meaning of "corporate responsibility." As His Holiness said, "I want a holistic perspective on business." After some seven years of meeting with one another we had found a way to synthesize the concepts of Buddhism with those of prominent Western thinkers to cope better with the dilemmas of business, and hence this book was born.

Buddhism and capitalism have their complexities and *The Leader's Way* inevitably simplifies both, while exploring their practical principles. The book is structured progressively: starting with the individual, leading to the company or organization, and culminating with society at large. A clear emphasis has been placed on leadership. Change makers are not exclusively found among top management and leaders, and we encourage employees at all levels to find the leader within and to employ the practices in this book.

Part I, "Leading Yourself," discusses the basics of Buddhism and how those unfamiliar with it can come to see the applicability of what the Buddha taught in all aspects of life. We emphasize the importance of good decision making, as well as the development of mental exercises that improve the performance of the mind. We also introduce some of the fundamental concepts of Buddhism.

In Part II, "Leading Your Organization," we take the ideas and values of Part I and show how they can be applied in the business framework. Leaders of organizations are encouraged to bring warmth, compassion, and ethics into their decision making and their policies and procedures; in their turn, companies are encouraged to look for leaders with integrity.

Part III, "Leading in an Interconnected World," then seeks to apply Buddhist values on a global scale and addresses the important topics of poverty, sustainability, diversity, and environmental responsibility. The aim is that even a small amount of change in our approach to these issues will foster hope and possibility.

The world today faces many challenges. Our total wealth has increased enormously and we are benefiting from technological miracles, but at the same time billions of people are living in abject poverty, we face the imminent threat of environmental disaster, and even those in prosperous nations feel insecure about the future. To address these problems requires a different kind of leadership, which sees things as they really are and can resolve them in a holistic way. That is what this book is about.

True leaders have the ability to look at an issue from many perspectives and, based on that expanded view, to make the right decisions. They have a calm, collected, and concentrated mind, undisturbed by negative thoughts and emotions, trained and focused. And true leadership recognizes the inevitability of change, the need for a sense of universal responsibility, and the importance of combining an economic system with moral values. *That* is the leader's way.

It is here that the ultimate wishes of the Dalai Lama – and myself – are expressed: that by improving the quality of our leaders' decisions, we will find ourselves in a better world for everyone.

PART I

LEADING
YOURSELF

*The best way for a ruler to reign over his country
is first of all to rule himself*

CHAPTER ONE

TAKING THE RIGHT VIEW

S OME PEOPLE HAVE the mistaken impression that Buddhism leads only to passivity, to people forsaking this materialistic world and meditating in the forest. In truth, this kind of isolation is intended primarily for monks and nuns. As a philosophy, Buddhism does deal with classic philosophical questions: What is truth and how can we ascertain it? What is the purpose of life? What is this universe in which we dwell? What are human nature, duty, and destiny? What is good and what is bad?

But the main emphasis of Buddhism is specifically on taking the right actions: What should I do? The essence of Buddhism can be summed up in the two concepts of Right View and Right Conduct. The Right View is of no value if it does not lead to the right action – and taking the right action is obviously fundamental for the success of business.

Leadership is about making decisions, and not just any decisions – the right ones. Leaders of global companies make decisions that affect thousands or even millions of people, and political leaders make decisions that affect tens of millions. Therefore making the right decisions is all important, as incompetent decision making can have disastrous effects.

The Buddhist view is that a true leader is one who makes the right decisions. That depends on taking the Right View and having what the Dalai Lama refers to as "a calm, collected, and concentrated mind," one that is peaceful, undisturbed by negative thoughts and emotions, trained, and focused. The purpose of this chapter is to introduce some central concepts of Buddhist philosophy and to show how, when adopted, they can improve the quality of our lives and our organizations.

To improve the quality of the decisions they make, leaders have to improve their minds. It is a central concept of Buddhism that every man and every woman can decide to improve his or her mind, and that doing so will lead to a happier life for themselves and others. You can improve your mind by thinking the right way and acting the right way. But you cannot act the right way if you do not *think* the right way.

Thinking the right way means thinking before every action to make sure that the action is based on the right intention and has the right motivation. The right intention is that the action will be beneficial to you and everyone affected by it; that is, it takes into account the wellbeing of self and others. This is true for individuals and for organizations.

Having the right intention is the first part of the Buddhist concept of Right View. The second part recognizes three aspects of reality: nothing exists that is permanent, everything changes; nothing exists that is independent; nothing exists without a cause. You may think that this is rather obvious, but people forget to take it into account when making decisions.

Recognizing interdependence and continuous change is also the basis of systems thinking in the West. Many prominent contributions have been made by academics at the Massachusetts Institute of Technology, for example Peter

Senge in organizational learning, Jay Forrester in systems dynamics, and Marvin Minsky's Society of Mind theory of human cognition. The Santa Fe Institute in New Mexico, with its many Nobel Prize winners such as Murray Gell-Mann and Kenneth Arrow, continues to advance knowledge on how a complex system like the economy, even society, functions. They all follow the same path: What are effects, and how do causes and effects interact? We use the word "holistic" with a similar meaning to systems thinking.

Thinking the right way depends on having a calm, collected, and concentrated mind. If your mind is influenced by anger, jealousy, fear, or lack of self-confidence, you become disturbed and inefficient; you cannot see reality; and your mind is no longer calm, collected, and concentrated. You have to develop the capability of *mindfulness*. Mindfulness means that you can see when a negative emotion starts to influence your mind. You also have to develop the ability to stop these negative emotions taking control over your mind. You have to gain and maintain control over the state of your mind to make your decisions according to Right View. In the next few chapters we explain how to train your mind in this way.

Right View relates to the intention behind a decision. Right Conduct, another Buddhist concept, refers to the quality of the *actions* a company and its employees take as a result of that decision. All of our actions should take into consideration their effect on others. We discuss Right Conduct in more detail in Chapter Two.

This book is unique in applying the principles of Right View and Right Conduct to decision making in organizations. An organization is not the sum of the individuals within it, it is both more and less. It is much more because the organization can accomplish many things that individuals alone cannot. It is much less because its members also have their private life, family, friends, and membership of other groups.

We do not want to give the impression or claim that applying Right View and Right Conduct is easy. It is not. Reaching perfection is beyond the capability of almost everyone. What we do claim is that everyone can improve their minds and performance if they want to. And that is also true for every organization, whether small, large, private sector, public sector, charity, not for profit, or NGO.

This book is not about Buddhism as a religion or as a way of life. The view of the Dalai Lama is that people can find values to help them lead a good and responsible life in all religious traditions. The Dalai Lama also believes that people who do not follow any religion can lead a good and responsible life. The ideas in this book are therefore possible for everyone to accept and practice.

At first sight you might expect a large difference between business and Buddhism, but their common denominator is the importance they attach to happiness. A company that does not have happy employees, customers, and shareholders will ultimately die. Buddha considered that the main purpose of his investigations and teachings was to find out the causes of a lack of happiness and what could be done to reduce suffering. His conclusion was that the root cause of suffering was self-centeredness. He referred to that as a law of nature.

Self-centeredness is also the cause of negative thoughts, which are heedless of the consequences they may have for others. Cheating, lying, hiding bad intentions, aggression, anger, arrogance, jealousy, malice, and resentment all qualify as negative thoughts or emotions. When you succeed in reducing the occurrence of such negativity, you will notice that your relationships with other people quickly improve. It is simple! People would rather deal with a person who is interested in their wellbeing than with someone who is only interested in him- or herself. Many people are totally blind to this point, however. When they meet someone, they try to impose their ideas and convince them of their excellence without any interest in the other person.

Once your eyes are open to the damage that can come from negative thoughts and emotions, most people recognize the value of controlling them. A useful step is to install an "early warning system," an inner voice that says, "You are getting into a state of mind that falls into the negative category. Be careful: Make sure that you do not lose control of your thought processes and emotions." Most importantly, you want to tell yourself, "Remember, if the negative thought process is very strong, do not make any significant or irreversible decisions at this moment."

Over time, it is possible for a person to reach a stage where negative thoughts and emotions no longer emerge, or do so very seldom. It takes years of practice, of course, but the rewards are plentiful.

In the above remarks by the Dalai Lama we see the promise of Buddhist teachings and how they might be applied in the business world. The business arena and the concepts of Buddhism seem, at first, to be an unlikely pairing. The former, primarily concerned with production, profit, and growth, seems to stand in contrast with the latter, which concerns itself with compassion for others and the wellbeing of humankind and our planet. Take a closer look, however, and we find that business practices and Buddhist principles are both concerned with happiness and making the right decisions. They are not such an awkward coupling; indeed, when working in concert they can address some of the foremost problems of our time. That, of course, is the premise of this book.

To expect rapid systematic change to the global economic system is unrealistic, and so incremental change must begin with individuals and individual businesses. It is the leaders of our world – in business, in government, in not-for-profit organizations – who can influence the path toward change for the rest of us. This is not to suggest that leaders are only at the "top" of an organization; leaders can be found among all ranks. We do suggest that unless the leaders at the top choose the right path, the leaders lower down in the organization cannot and will not go the right way.

RIGHT VIEW: DEVELOPING WISDOM

Right View consists of two parts: the decision-making process and the three values or concepts that have to be respected in every decision. Leaders are faced all the time by the necessity to make decisions. When difficult circumstances arise, either on a personal or a company level, the goal is not to respond from a self-centered point of view but from the point of view of the company and all the people and organizations affected by the decision. Our concern is that the *process* – from originating the decision to taking the action and following up its effects – functions in the best possible way. The focus in decision making according to Right View is always on what the *effects* will be after implementation.

The first point to consider in the decision-making process is the *intention* behind the action under consideration. The intention must be good, meaning that as a minimum it results in no harm to others. In some cases an action is beneficial to some and unavoidably detrimental to others. Nevertheless, the utmost effort should be made through creativity and innovation to reduce the harm as much as possible. Throughout this book we will give many examples of the right kind of decision-making processes.

The second point is the *state of mind* of the leader and, as far as possible, also that of the other people involved in the process. The challenge for the decision maker is to recognize the origination of any negative effects on the mind such as defensiveness or anger, and to be able to return the mind to a calm, collected, and concentrated state.

When coming to the end of the decision-making process, leaders should ask themselves: Are the *effects* of this decision beneficial for my organization and also for any others concerned? What is my motivation: Am I only seeking a benefit for myself or did I also consider the benefits for others?

The cause-and-effect aspect of decision making can be better understood through the Buddhist principles of dependent origination, interdependence, and impermanence, each of which His Holiness explains as follows.

Dependent origination (causes and conditions) is another way of stating the principle of causality: the law of cause and effect, of action and consequence. Nothing exists without a cause and nothing changes of its own accord.

There is nothing new in this principle, but thorough awareness of it makes a difference for the following reasons. A decision initiates change. To that change there will be innumerable reactions, some positive and some negative. However competent the decision maker and however much he has trained his mind, no leader can foresee all the effects that originate from their actions. But leaders who have the right intention and are very thorough in thinking through the effects of their decisions will make fewer mistakes.

In this context two other principles are important: seeing the way things really are, and looking at consequences from the point of view of others and from many perspectives. We will return to the application of these principles throughout the book.

There is a small but interesting difference between "classic" cause and effect and dependent origination. In dependent origination the emphasis is on the *process* between the cause and the effect. When studying the process, particular attention is paid to the conditions that made the event's occurrence possible as well as the conditions on which the effect depended. The success of the decision always depends on many conditions, and these have to be analyzed too.

I offered this straightforward example of dependent origination to the Dalai Lama: Imagine a high-level executive who discovers that a peer in another company, one that is smaller and less successful, is receiving higher compensation than he is. His natural reaction is to judge this as unfair. (It would be unnatural if he were proud of earning a lower salary than a less successful person.) His thought process then leads to the question, "What should I do, if anything?" Someone who is unaware of the concepts of Right View and Right Conduct is likely to contact the board of directors and point out that he is underpaid, suggesting that a compensation consultant be engaged to analyze the situation and determine a fair level of compensation for him. He does not consider any ripple effects that his action may have on others.

On the other hand, a business leader who is aware of Right View and Right Conduct – who has a trained mind, as discussed further in Chapters Two and Three – thinks differently. He asks, "Is my mind influenced by greed? Am I starting out on a path that is self-centered?" He may stop the process immediately, or he may proceed with great care. He may reflect on the fact that he earns far more than is necessary to live comfortably. As part of this reflection, a thought may creep into his mind that many businesspeople in similar positions have, let's say, skiing lodges in Aspen. He immediately recognizes this as the start of a thought process tainted by jealousy. He then asks himself, "How would my request affect the rest of the company?" This is a typical example of being mindful of negative thoughts and emotions. He remembers that the company has recently suffered layoffs. Would it be fair to ask for more money? Would morale suffer? This kind of questioning of the effect of his actions on others continues until he reaches his decision.

In the end, the decision may be to raise the issue of unfair compensation with his superiors, or it may not be; but either way, the person with the trained mind analyzes the consequences of his action and is aware that he should watch carefully for self-centered motivation and emotions such as jealousy.

Of course, decisions become more complex when we move beyond the example of the single executive to the level of the corporation. When corporations make decisions, the effect has to be foreseen down the line for many reasons: financial risks; a company's reputation; and to consider whether it is the best action to take for the majority of employees and for all the other stakeholders.

Interdependence is cause and effect from a different perspective. As nothing exists without a cause and every cause has many effects, interdependence between different phenomena is the logical consequence. Here it means focusing on our dependence on each other. All actions have effects on self and on others. My actions have an effect on other people. Their reaction to my action has an effect on me, and so on in an endless chain.

A company is a typical example of an interdependent organization. It depends on customers, government policies, and political developments, on its employees, customers, shareholders, and distributors – actions and reactions in an endless chain.

The jewelry net of Indra provides a beautiful image of interdependence.[1] Indra was the Hindu god of the universe. He used a net in the shape of a ball. At each knot is a jewel. When a jewel emits light it is reflected in all the other jewels. The reflections are returned to the emitting jewel and go back again. Imagine you are one of the jewels. You the other people and the net as a whole are constantly changing in an interdependent system.

Leaders realize their dependence on others, but often do not fully understand how dependent they are on the reaction of other people outside their control, customers and the media for example. The best leaders are very aware of the importance of these interactions for their reputation: One serious mistake and it takes decades to rebuild a tarnished reputation.

Impermanence is another consequence of cause and effect. Given innumerable causes and effects, nothing exists that is permanent and without a cause. This concept leads to a great deal of confusion as in Buddhist literature it is referred to as "emptiness." This is an abbreviation of "Empty of anything that exists inherently"; that is, without a cause, totally independent. This can also be expressed differently: The only things that exist are processes operating in a network of causes and effects. People know this to be true but do not like it; they would prefer permanent satisfactory states.

Many business leaders make the same mistake. They fix goals and objectives and hope that when reached these will lead to a permanent satisfactory state. That is impossible. Every goal is a moving target.

Leaders and everybody else must recognize that a myriad of developments will occur that make it impossible to reach a steady-state goal of satisfaction without making changes, some pleasant and others not so pleasant. We all have to face reality and make many changes. This is one of the greatest challenges in society today, how to cope with an increasing rate of change. Even companies that have been successful over many years will not continue to be successful for ever.

> Impermanence (or "constant change") shows up everywhere in the business world. It is a familiar refrain for today's business leaders. Robert H. Rosen, founder of Healthy Companies International, puts it this way:
>
> *While traveling through Asia, I was especially struck by the Buddhist notion of impermanence. The idea is that change is the natural state of things, everything in life grows and decays, and uncertainty and anxiety are an inherent part of being alive… I began looking beyond the office of the leaders I was meeting to see real men and women, with personal aspirations, vulnerabilities, and fears. I began to see how we all live with some degree of anxiety over much of our lives.[2]*

Corporations depend on innovation, reinventing the company, rebranding products, and finding ways to remain competitive in the global marketplace and satisfy changing customer requirements. For these reasons, of all the Buddhist concepts, impermanence is the one that is most readily understood by the business world. But even though they understand it, many businesses react too slowly, do not catch the next innovation wave, or introduce new products too late.

You may wonder why there is a need to have three concepts that are basically the same. Experience over several millennia shows that each concept activates different parts of the mind, so you gain a more thorough understanding of reality. Just try!

The Buddhist view is not fatalistic — it does not suggest that we accept change for the worse as a fact of life. On the contrary, by being aware of constant change and trying to spot negative change at an early stage, negative developments can be avoided and sometimes become positive opportunities. Businesses should continually search for positive ways to deal with change.

Buddhism stresses that the three concepts of cause and effect, interdependence, and impermanence must move beyond intellectual understanding. They must become "realizations"; they must be experienced at the level of feelings and become an integral part of the mind.

As long as we live in this world we are bound to encounter problems. If, at such times, we lose hope and become discouraged, we diminish our ability to face difficulties. If, on the other hand, we remember that it is not just ourselves but everyone who has to undergo suffering, this more realistic perspective will increase our determination and capacity to overcome troubles. Indeed, with this attitude, each new obstacle can be seen as yet another valuable opportunity to improve the mind.

This book is designed to help business leaders develop the ability to look at an issue from many perspectives – short term, long term, from the points of view of different stakeholders – and then to use that expanded view to make the right decisions.

ACCEPTING REALITY, STAYING POSITIVE

So, it is the Buddhist approach that to understand reality fully – to see and accept things the way they really are – a person must accept Right View and have considerable control over negative emotions such as anger or jealousy. Two phenomena that are often obstacles to seeing reality are wishful thinking and thinking about problems of the past as if they still exist today.

Wishful thinking is quite common in business. The marketplace requires businesspeople to make progress, to have confidence in their direction. A businessperson with a pessimistic nature is unlikely to succeed. However, the desire to be successful leads many businesspeople to reject negative information. A clear example of this is when employees experience a problem in the workplace and wait a long time to bring it to the attention of their manager. They may be hoping that the problem will go away on its own so they do not have to be a messenger of bad news. When they see a colleague getting involved in something very negative like corruption, they are reluctant to report it as they fear, rightly so in many cases, that they will be punished. Situations like these arise quite often and illustrate why top management is so often unaware of problems until they have become very serious and difficult to correct. Consider this maxim employed by one company: "Good news must travel slowly, bad news should travel quickly."[3] Adopting this frame of mind helps companies remain better informed of potential problems before they become liabilities. It is an effective way to become aware of reality before it is too late.

Thinking about problems of the past as if they are reality today is another way to express this concept of transferring experiences of the past into the present. If a negative thought process is allowed to take hold, a great deal of energy is wasted on being upset and angry about a past event. Many businesspeople fall into the trap of spending emotional energy on injustices that they or their companies have suffered in the past. Dwelling on the past as if it were the present is counterproductive, it is a waste of time.

Take the story of Thitinart na Patalung, chief executive of Working Diamond in Thailand. Thitinart described how she had been very successful in business but had lost everything when her business partner cheated her. As a result, she became very depressed and angry. At the suggestion of a friend, however, she decided to attend a meditation course. When she started her meditation, one of the first things that entered her mind was the face of this disloyal partner, and she became furious on the spot. After calming herself down, she was able to analyze her thought process. She started to realize that she was experiencing something as "real" that was only a mental process, without any independent existence. She was conjuring up the betrayal in her mind over and over again. She compared the development of this intense anger about past events to someone holding a piece of broken glass in their hand and squeezing the glass until their hand bleeds, then squeezing some more and producing more blood. She found that realizing that the anger she experienced only existed in her mind enabled her to get rid of her bitterness about the past.

Decisions are made primarily to change something. Change is often thought of as moving from one situation to another, but this is a dangerous simplification. The present situation is the result of innumerable causes and conditions; it is also dependent on many causes and conditions. It is changing all the time and it is impermanent. Recognizing these interdependencies and interconnections inspires a wholesome state of humility within us; it causes us to accept the complexity of making a successful change. It also should lead to a holistic rather than narrow-minded view of change. In other words, before a decision is made, consider the consequences from many different perspectives. Acceptance of impermanence should also strengthen your resolve to monitor how decisions are executed.

Right View is a fairly easy concept to understand, but applying it properly requires skill. Every situation is unique and there are no automatic answers. Having a grasp of the principles is the first step, but the decision maker still has to think a great deal, learn how to cope with conflicting objectives, weigh short- and long-term consequences, and consider different interest groups. Using these concepts requires practice, and with practice comes skill.

Developing the Right View is the foundation on which the remainder of the concepts in this book are based. It is impossible to achieve positive change with the wrong view.

The following chapters explain how to combine Right View with its twin concept of Right Conduct, and show the value of finding a disciplined practice that works for you and your particular circumstances. Keep Right View and Right Conduct always active in your mind, and good decision making will then follow.

CHAPTER TWO

DOING THE RIGHT THING

I N BUDDHISM WE consider it very important that people teaching Buddhist principles apply them in their own conduct. In India at the time of Buddha, teachers and philosophers were only taken seriously if they lived as they preached. Although most of the teachings of Buddha are very clear, moving from theory to practice when it comes to human behavior requires determination and effort. Mastering their application completely is a target to strive for.

For true leaders the same principle applies as to these early philosophers. A leader will only be respected when he acts according to the principles in which he says he believes. Or, to put it differently, many people imitate the behavior of their leaders. If that behavior is different from the stated principles, people will follow the behavior and not the principles.

In Buddhism a person is considered to be the accumulation of all of his actions up to that point in time. Good actions make a person good, bad actions bad. The effect of bad actions can be reduced by subsequent good actions. This is referred to as the law of karma.

In Chapter One we saw that the quality of decision making depends on using the principles of Right View and on the skill and energy with which these principles are applied. Through determination and practice (also known as training the mind), anyone can achieve a greater ability to choose the right path. This is particularly effective for leaders as they decide what to do for their organizations and the people who work for them. These decisions take the form of policies and practices as well as the functional roles that individuals play. In plain terms, managers must serve the needs of the whole organization as well as those of individual workers.

It often seems that leaders are put in a no-win situation, as these needs can be at odds with one another. The Dalai Lama's answer to that conundrum would be this. The principle is simple: the effect of the decision should be beneficial to the organization and to any others affected. Harm is to be avoided. In reality, a decision may produce benefits for some but represent disadvantages for others. In such a case, choose the way that gives benefits to the largest number of people.

The situation is even more difficult when it is impossible to avoid harming some people. The Buddhist principle is that if harm cannot be avoided, it must eliminate a much greater harm to other people. There is a three-stage decision-making process. Make your initial decision and check whether the result is any harm to anyone. If no, you can go ahead. If yes, apply your creativity to find another solution that eliminates the harm. If it is completely impossible to avoid harm of some sort, then you have to make certain that this harm is justified because it avoids a much greater harm, or because it leads to huge benefits for some other people. For example, if a company is in a financial crisis because its sales have fallen dramatically, it can justify laying people off. Those people will be harmed, but the jobs of the people remaining employed will be saved. Of course it would have been better if the crisis had been avoided in the first place, but crises do happen.

A good leader must develop the capability to deal with such situations so that people both inside and outside the organization consider the decisions made to be fair ones. It is not enough that the decision is fair, though: the leader must also communicate the rationale for the decision in an effective way to the people concerned.

Making decisions and taking action are critical parts of leadership. However, not just any action will do. Often managers make decisions for the sake of "ticking a box," but this is a faulty tactic. This chapter describes how the actions taken must be wholesome ones, meaning that they are ethical in nature and arise from an awareness of Right View and a trained mind. Out of these ethical decisions, advises the Buddha, comes peace. Not taking action can be an unwholesome act in itself, in that sometimes standing by can bring about suffering. So, how does one learn when, and how, to take the right action?

TAKING ETHICAL ACTIONS

After Kenneth Lay, former chief executive of Enron, was convicted in 2006 of fraud and conspiracy charges, one of his collaborators made the following remark: "We want honest leaders who are decisive, creative, optimistic and even courageous. But often we don't even look for one of the most critical traits of a leader: humility."[1] A humble leader listens to others. He or she values input from employees, even if it is bad news, and humility is marked by an ability to admit mistakes.

Most people would say that some measure of humility is an essential trait of a leader. But there are other characteristics as well – kindness, a sense of equanimity, even self-confidence – that are considered to be important in Buddhism. These are best described as "wholesome" and "unwholesome" actions and attitudes; and there is a recommended process for "throwing out" (ejecting) the bad ones and "welcoming in" (replacing them with) the good.

In Buddhism we have the concept of wholesome and unwholesome tendencies (in thought and action). Wholesome actions lead to physical and moral wellbeing and could be thought of as ethical actions; unwholesome actions result in suffering and harm and can, therefore, be seen as unethical. Furthermore, people have both wholesome and unwholesome tendencies. The task is therefore to remove the unwholesome tendencies and fill the vacated space with wholesome tendencies. An important point is that wholesome and unwholesome actions and thoughts are mutually exclusive: A person cannot be angry and calm at the same time, or concentrated and distracted at the same time.

For our purposes here, we are focusing on the contrast between wholesome and unwholesome mental factors.[2] (Throughout the book, we will also refer to these factors as "positive" and "negative" emotions.) If we combine the wholesome and unwholesome factors in pairs, it becomes easy to see what we should get rid of – eject – and which one to put in its place. We give a couple of examples here; you can find the remaining pairs at the end of the chapter.

The ejection procedure for all unwholesome mental factors is the same. The first step is to carry out analytical meditation (discussed in Chapter Three) on a given attitude – to think about it — and draw conclusions as to whether it is making a constructive contribution. The second step is to apply one-pointed meditation (also in Chapter Three) to that conclusion in order to replace the emotion with a positive one. These two steps have to be repeated many times. Then over time the ejecting and replacing process becomes more natural.

Although these factors may seem removed from the business world, in fact that is not the case. If leaders in business replace unhealthy mental attitudes with healthy ones, better leadership follows at once. The age-old phrase "Lead by example" is at work here. Rather than telling members of their organization how to act or what to do, a leader with a trained mind becomes the one to emulate. This framework gives a very comprehensive starting point.

Self-confidence ejects lack of self-confidence

According to Buddha, the greatest treasure humans can have is self-confidence. We expect leaders and heads of companies to be self-confident but they may just appear that way; for many this is a façade. Leaders often suffer from lack of confidence because they are not sure that what they are doing is right. In my view, lack of self-confidence is a waste of time because it does not contribute to finding the right solutions. To combat this, leaders must apply the concept of dependent origination in everyday life (see Chapter One). By that I mean that they must make wise decisions by taking all factors into account. Once those in charge start thinking in this interconnected way, they feel the rightness of their actions — and self-confidence builds from there.

Heedfulness and concentration eject distraction, carelessness, thoughtlessness, and forgetfulness

Heedfulness means, quite simply, playing close attention. People are quite perceptive in their ability to judge this quality. If you are not listening to someone when you are in conversation with them, the chances are that they will know and communication becomes all but impossible. Giving your full attention to the other person is considered not only good manners but also ethical or wholesome.

"Heedfulness" is particularly important, even inspiring, in a leader. If a leader truly listens to you, it makes you feel valued, important.

Take the Dalai Lama, for example. I have met hundreds of busy people over the years, but few if any with as large a workload as he. But when I speak with him, I feel that he has one hundred percent concentration on what I am saying. We've never been interrupted by a phone call or people coming in to speak with him, and yet I know that his time is very valuable. If a leader can convey a similar sense that all the people in their care are that important to them, trust is the result. And out of trust come all kinds of possibilities.

The process of learning how to eject the unwanted action and replace it with the desired one is useful for any individual. It will seem an obvious point that if unwholesome factors and emotions are ejected and replaced by wholesome factors, more time can be spent on productive mental activity, and there will be less suffering and more wellbeing as a result. There can be more "getting on with it" and less "cleaning up" after poor decisions have been made. To implement the process requires developing a certain skill set: the power of observation, the practice of discipline, and a fair dose of patience as well.

VALUING RIGHT LIVELIHOOD

One of the main decisions we make is how to earn a living. The concept of right livelihood means that one should earn one's living in a righteous way and that wealth should be gained legally and peacefully. The Buddha mentions four specific activities that harm other beings and that one should avoid for this reason: dealing in weapons; dealing in living beings (including raising animals for slaughter as well as the slave trade and prostitution); working in meat production and butchery; and selling intoxicants and poisons, such as alcohol and drugs. Furthermore, any other occupation that would violate the principles of Right Conduct should be avoided.

The definition of right livelihood as "acting in a righteous way legally and peacefully" presents the main principles. The four specific activities deserve some comment.

I strongly believe that war is wrong, but that it was justified when the allies liberated Europe and Asia from German and Japanese occupation. Then arms were essential. In all circumstances everything possible should be done to avoid the necessity of using arms.

Dealing in human beings is of course wrong, but raising animals for slaughter and meat production are commonplace in all countries. Most but not all Buddhist monks are vegetarians. I was raised as a vegetarian, but after a serious illness doctors told me I had to eat some meat, which I have continued since.

Selling illegal drugs is obviously wrong, but selling intoxicants such as alcohol is common in all countries. This poses a similar problem as with meat, the question of freedom. Attempts to ban the sale of intoxicants have never worked well and lead to a black market. These problems have to be solved by the education of buyers, they cannot be solved by forbidding sales.

With these caveats, someone who acts with the right intentions, Right View, and Right Conduct is likely to earn his or her living in the right way.

THE SIX PERFECTIONS

The Six Perfections — often expressed as generosity, ethical discipline, patience, enthusiastic effort, concentration, and wisdom — are of obvious value to all individuals, not just leaders. But a leader who possesses these traits has a distinct ability to affect others in profound ways.

Generosity
The cause of many business scandals is the greed of those in power, greed for money and prestige; quite the opposite of generosity. Even though good performance by the chief executive is essential for the success of the company, the actual results are achieved through the collaboration of everyone within the organization. A leader who wants to take all the credit destroys other people's motivation. A good chief executive must be very generous in giving credit where it is due. Most leaders of successful organizations are in fact modest people who attribute good results to their team.

Generosity should be combined with wisdom. To be generous in solving only a short-term problem is not acceptable. Generosity must consider short- and long-term effects.

Ethical discipline
When I think of ethical discipline, I am reminded of the advice given to other rulers by a king who was notably successful in governing his realm. He explained the principle of his adminis-

tration as follows: "The best way for a ruler to reign over his country is first of all to rule himself." By "ruling himself" he meant withstanding temptation. Most kings want to be rich, admired, respected, and successful. Unless the actions to reach such objectives are governed by moral restraint, the result will be trouble in the kingdom. That is why we refer not just to "discipline," but also to "ethical discipline." It is not wrong to become wealthy if the wealth is earned honestly and without harming others or the environment, but it is not acceptable that a person at the head of a company should become very wealthy while the company itself collapses, resulting in shareholders losing their savings and employees their jobs.

This is not to say that self-discipline is easy to achieve. I often refer to ethical discipline as "taming the mind." An undisciplined mind is like an elephant. If left to blunder around out of control, it will wreak havoc. The main problem is to get control of our negative motivations and emotions such as greed, self-centeredness, anger, hatred, lust, fear, lack of self-confidence, and jealousy. We can conceive of the nature of the mind in terms of water in a lake. When the water is stirred up (by negative thoughts or emotions), mud from the lake's bottom clouds it. When the storm has passed, the mud settles and the water (the mind) is left clear again. The "storm" refers to the effect of negative motivations and emotions. Prior to every action, we should rid ourselves of all negative thoughts, so that we are "free" to respond. Until we have learned to discipline our minds, we will have difficulty exercising this freedom.

Patience

Patience must be cultivated. It is the only way to be prepared when provocative circumstances occur, such as hostility, criticism, or disappointment. In the case of anger, it is not the ability to suppress it but the ability to remain calm in the face of it that counts. To do so requires training the mind, which leads to a calm, patient mind.

Patience should be understood as "justified patience." In some cases immediate action is necessary. Deciding whether or not to exercise patience requires good judgment.

Enthusiastic effort

Our level of enthusiasm depends on our belief in the importance of the goals we want to reach and our motivation to get there. We've heard it said that "Enthusiasm is contagious," meaning that people have enormous reserves of energy that can be mobilized with enthusiasm. Being able to encourage this enthusiasm is an essential trait in a leader.

Concentration

By concentration I refer to the ability to focus all your mental energy on one issue. Most people have very poor concentration, bouncing from one thing to the next. They waste a lot of time thinking about things that went wrong in the past, worrying about the future, about problems with employees and family. Leaders are not immune to this. However, people who cannot concentrate are unable to focus their mind, which is essential for improving the quality of their decisions.

Wisdom

Wisdom is essentially possessing Right View — the ability to see things as they are and the realization that nothing is permanent. Deciding what has to be done today to safeguard the long-term future requires Right View and Right Conduct.

REAPING THE BENEFITS

I interviewed many executives in Asia who are very enthusiastic about the benefits they gain from applying the principles of Right View and Right Conduct, and from training the mind through meditation, as we outline in Chapter Three.

For instance, a decade ago Thai business leaders were facing an economic crisis. Several came close to declaring bankruptcy. Nevertheless, under such conditions those who were practicing Buddhists noted that compared to colleagues in other companies, they had been able to react to this adversity with a greater sense of calm and with clear deliberation. They were asked about their views of the purpose of business. None answered that the primary goals involved profit or shareholder value. One manager, who was responsible for a very profitable company, commented, "The main weakness of managers in the West is that they are too concerned about the bottom line. In all my business dealings I make sure that my customers get a good deal... but also our company. Profit comes as a result."

The managers were able to characterize their skills as follows:

❖ *Increased ability to deal with a crisis*. One manager said that almost all of the managers in the same sector had gone to the banks to ask for some forgiveness of debt. He was one of the few who had not tried. He admitted to having been very worried, but opted instead to talk with his Buddhist teacher. The teacher told him, "I understand nothing of your problems, but if you calm down and meditate, I am sure you will find a solution." At first this may have been seen as dismissive, but the manager followed his advice successfully.

❖ *Better decision making.* The managers said that they agonized less about making the wrong decisions and felt that they had a better frame of reference within which to make decisions. They found it easier to concentrate on the issues and had become more self-confident in their choices.

❖ *Better relations with the people directly reporting to them.* The Buddhist leaders ascribed their good relations to more patience when dealing with controversy or employee relations issues. They described a willingness to look at an issue several times, and did not feel threatened by appearing indecisive at first.

❖ *Fewer meetings and better execution of decisions.* Several of the CEOs reported that fewer meetings were required because they had learned to give their undivided attention to the item at hand. They listened more carefully to colleagues when decisions were being made and when the execution of those decisions was discussed.

❖ *More creativity.* This was explained in an interesting way by the head of an architectural firm in Taiwan, Kris Yao. He described his increased creativity as a result of his mind training: "Before I started mind training, like most architects I was very keen on designing something unique, different from what others were doing. I hoped that people seeing my buildings would admire their unique beauty and that I might become one of the famous architects." Yao had accompanied the Dalai Lama on one of his visits to Taiwan and had become inspired by Buddhist ideas. He said, "I have let go of that ambition and instead concentrate on what is best for the client and the people that will 'live in' the building. I found that my creativity increased. My clients are more satisfied than before and I am more satisfied too."

❖ *A high level of enthusiasm for their job.* All of these leaders were enthusiastic about their job and about the benefits they felt they had experienced from being active Buddhists and training their mind. This enthusiasm pervaded their work.

The managers in the above examples understood and practiced Right Conduct and Right View, no doubt because they have systematically begun to change their thought processes and resulting behaviors. If you examine these examples closely, the benefits that result from these leaders' actions are all due to a reduction in unwholesome mental factors. Their view that "Buddhism has no impact on action unless you practice" is very telling. What they are getting at is that change is cultivated over time once you begin to replace poorer actions with better ones. It is encouraging to know that Buddhism has a great deal of knowledge to bring to the modern corporation – and to the global economy.

To make real progress you have to change the way you act and the organization in which you work has to change too. This can be done successfully by applying the principles of Right View and Right Conduct. Right View means that you will at all times be actively concerned not only for your own wellbeing but also for that of others. Right Conduct means that you accept the hard work necessary to apply the principles of Right View. True leaders will choose this disciplined path to bring these practices into their places of work.

WELCOMING IN THE GOOD

Here are the remaining pairs of wholesome and unwholesome mental factors, where through meditation you can throw out the bad and welcome in the good.

Humility ejects unjustified pride, inflated self-esteem, conceit, and arrogance

Having humility may appear to be the opposite of self-confidence. However, for people who experience continued success, self-confidence can deteriorate into unjustified (or false) pride. When leaders start to think that all their successes are due to their own brilliance and decisiveness, they have lost a sense of humility and instead have inflated self-esteem. They forget that their success depends on many other people — and probably on some luck as well. The important point here is to remember that no success is solely yours and to remain humble in the face of it. People can recognize humility instantly in a leader and find it an inspiring trait.

Consideration and active concern for the wellbeing of others eject lack of consideration for others, meanness, and harming others

Being concerned for the wellbeing of others is very close to the overall concept of Right Conduct: Every action we take should consider its effect on others. Consideration is on this list because it is one of the wholesome factors; however, beyond being a positive characteristic of leaders, it should also become a state of mind. Anyone, but particularly a leader in society, should come to consider the wellbeing of others first and foremost, no matter what decision they are facing.

Equanimity…
Equanimity essentially means calmness of mind and is a very important mental factor. It is in fact better described as evenness of emotion; one who has equanimity is seen as open-minded, peaceful, and without bias. Equanimity is often referred to as the absence of attachment to desire or craving. Imagine a leader who exudes this quality. Although this may not conjure up a dynamic driver of a business, it portrays a person you can trust – arguably the most essential quality of leadership.

…ejects craving for power, wealth, and fame
There is nothing wrong with desiring wealth if it is honestly earned, or with fame when a person makes a positive contribution. Nonattachment and desire are words that can be easily misconstrued. For example, desire can be positive if it is used for achieving a wholesome state of mind, but negative when it refers to desiring wealth. When referring to the negative aspect, we therefore use the word "craving," which refers to a person who is driven by an insatiable desire for wealth or fame. As there are always more famous and wealthier people, a person with such a craving will never be happy. Even worse is that people with such cravings are likely to take shortcuts to achieve their aims, including harming others and breaking laws. People who do not control their cravings have become slaves of this unwholesome emotion.

…ejects dejection or worry when failing to reach objectives or experiencing disappointments
It is natural for managers to be worried when one of their best collaborators leaves, when it is discovered that the

company has been involved in price fixing without them knowing, or if the company has to report a loss instead of a profit. Worry is a waste of energy, however. It does not solve anything. To get rid of worry is not easy. But meditating on the uselessness of it and dropping the emotion as soon as it manifests itself, without violently suppressing it, eventually will lead to equanimity.

...ejects hatred, anger, wrath, resentment, spite, envy, and jealousy

The emotions of anger, hatred, and resentment can be very strong and are unproductive, waste energy, can cause suffering, and may lead to distraction. The method for ejecting these time-wasting energies is much the same as with worry. By using meditation and by considering the uselessness of these emotions, you can move beyond them into the desired state of equanimity, or a feeling of composure or calmness of mind.

A sense of shame ejects shamelessness

Shame may look like a strange factor on this list, as it is often thought of as a negative emotion. People sometimes make mistakes; that is unavoidable. I consider shame to be positive, however, when it leads to corrective action. And the absence of shame is dangerous, as it means that a person lacks minimal moral standards. In this context, though, guilt is less useful than shame. Guilt appears to be something permanent, about which nothing can be done. From that point of view it is unwholesome. It is better to turn guilt into shame, which in turn leads to remedial action. Buddhists believe that bad actions will have inevitable negative consequences on the person who committed the action. The only way to reduce these negative consequences is to counter them with good actions.

Kindness ejects indifference, hostility, irritability, ill-humor, and dislike

When I meet someone I always think of that person as a fellow human being and as someone who wants to be happy, like me. If the person acts in a hostile or unfriendly manner, I try to differentiate between the way they are acting and the person themselves. Buddhists believe that within every person is a wholesome or pure core, and that by extending kindness and friendship, hostility is diminished. Nothing can be gained by being unfriendly, though it is not necessary to withhold comment if a person is acting wrongly or holds wrong views. When confronted with the negative emotions of hostility and indifference, leaders should attempt to remedy the situation with kindness. It is the leader and only the leader who can successfully introduce and implement these concepts in his organization.

Vigor replaces dullness of mind or sloth

Striving for vigor is not likely to be a problem for leaders, as a high energy level is necessary to cope with the demands of their heavy workload. Without vigor an executive cannot succeed. However, for a company to succeed this energy must spread throughout the ranks. It is a challenge for leaders to find the best ways to promote it, by example and through specific policies.

Receptivity and an open mind eject fanaticism and blind faith

Flexibility or having an open mind is very important among the wholesome mental factors. More and more, flexibility is needed in the business world: flexibility for retaining good employees as well as for making business decisions that involve discussions between many people. There are few absolute truths. A leader should be careful about becoming fanatical, and equally avoid the organization acquiring fanatical traits. A company leader should inspire faith in the purpose of the organization – in a purpose that people believe to be right – and see to it that the company's values are respected by everyone. On the other hand, this process should not go too far. It is a question of finding the right balance.

CHAPTER THREE

TRAINING YOUR MIND

APPLYING THE PRINCIPLES of Right View and Right Conduct is a major challenge. Only a very gifted leader will be able to do so perfectly without training his or her mind.

I have trained my mind since I was very young. I still continue to do so, every day for several hours, both when I travel and when I am at home. My experience is that training the mind becomes a habit, like eating meals.

The good news is that you can make progress with a very modest investment of time. Reaching perfection is beyond the capabilities of almost everyone, therefore the main point is to aim for steady progress.

The challenges a leader faces and the number of potentially difficult decisions that have to be made within a limited amount of time can be daunting. The purpose of training the mind is to see to it that the mind is calm, collected, and concentrated in all circumstances. Another purpose is to enable the mind to analyze decisions quickly from many perspectives. That requires an open and supple mind; a closed and rigid mind will not do.

The untrained mind can be compared to a monkey swinging from branch to branch, wandering from one subject to another, without concentration. When the mind is disturbed by anger, jealousy, hate, impatience, fear, lack of self-confidence, or becoming emotional about negative things that happened in the past, the mind is wasting valuable thinking time. These negative thoughts and emotions take up time that instead should be used for constructive thinking. The purpose of training the mind is to maximize its power and concentrate on the decisions that matter.

For those more familiar with Western psychology than Eastern philosophy, the process of training the mind is also sometimes referred to as "conditioning," meaning that behavior becomes dependent on an event in the environment. For example, if you get angry and defensive as soon as you are criticized, you can condition yourself instead to listen attentively and analyze whether there is something to learn from the situation. Your actions depend on the conclusion you reach. The automatic reaction of becoming defensive when criticized is therefore replaced by the automatic reaction of listening with an open mind. To put it another way, conditioning your mind has changed your automatic reaction to criticism.

Over hundreds of years Buddhists have developed a large number of exercises to train the mind. In the second part of this chapter we will present seven exercises in a sequence of increasing complexity that ordinary people who are not specialists or Buddhists can practice. Before that, I want to review several questions that are frequently asked about training the mind.

HOW CAN YOU FIND TIME TO MEDITATE?

Anyone, including a busy executive, can find five minutes a day for the mental exercises outlined in this chapter. There are many ways to find time to practice. The delays of business life – waiting in an airport or a taxi, for example – are all opportunities to incorporate your practice into your daily life. Instead of being irritated, count these occasions as excellent opportunities for training the mind.

I used to be very uncomfortable when I had to wait. If I arrived at the airport and saw that there were long queues, it immediately made me nervous. Once in a queue I would worry that I should have chosen another, faster-moving line. I finally concluded that my behavior was silly and I adopted another way of looking at it. Now when I see a long queue, I think of it as a perfect opportunity for training my mind.

Remember that short stretches of five minutes, although not optimal times for meditation, do still have value. Many Buddhist executives have found ways to incorporate meditation into their daily lives at work. It need not be disruptive to the flow of activity, but can rather be introduced when moments of calm or clarity are called for.

SHOULD YOU TRAIN ON YOUR OWN OR WITH A TEACHER?

Seeking a qualified spiritual teacher is an important step in one's spiritual life.[1] But before accepting someone as your spiritual teacher, you must examine that person thoroughly. In Tibet we say, "Don't act like a dog finding a lump of meat." You should observe the teacher first, not just choose someone with an important title and widespread influence. A teacher is your guide on the spiritual path, and therefore he (or she) should practice what he teaches. Real guidance can be provided only from the teacher's own experience and not on the basis of mere intellectual understanding. The teacher should at least be gentle and have tamed his own mind, because the very purpose of adopting someone as your spiritual master is to tame your mind. The teacher should be someone who can answer your questions directly and help you to clarify your doubts.

Once you have accepted someone as your teacher, it is essential to cultivate a proper sense of faith and respect and abide by his instructions. It is important to be clear that faith and respect do not imply blind faith. The Buddha explained that a pupil should heed the teacher's virtuous instructions but disregard "unwholesome" commands. He pointed out the importance of people being skeptical about what teachers teach. Buddha, the greatest of teachers, said to his students:

Just as people test the purity of gold by burning it in fire, by cutting it and examining it on a touchstone, so exactly you should do, accept my words after subjecting them to a critical test and not out of reverence for me.

There are two ways to approach Buddhist teachings, the intelligent way and the unintelligent way. The intelligent way is to approach the scriptures and their commentaries with skepticism and an open mind, and to try to relate them to your own experience and understanding. Such a student will not follow a teaching or a scripture because it is attributed to a famous master. Rather, the validity of the content will be judged on the basis of that student's own understanding, derived through personal investigation and analysis. The intelligent way can be expressed as follows: "Rely on the message of the teacher, not on the person of the teacher. Rely on the meaning, not just on the words."

You can practice the walking, breathing, and mantra-citing techniques described at the end of this chapter without a teacher. One-pointed and analytical meditation are more difficult. I tried on my own by studying texts, even buying a tape, but it did not work. When I attended a retreat in Thailand I found that learning in a group makes it easier. That is surprising in a way, because you do not talk for a whole week to any of the participants. But sitting on the floor in the same room with many others all trying to meditate gave me extra force. The fact of spending an entire week learning something and only talking for 15 minutes a day to monks also had a positive effect.

Learning these techniques does require patience. Making some progress is relatively easy, but becoming really proficient in one-pointed and analytical meditation takes many years.

THE EFFECT OF MEDITATION ON THE BRAIN

Recent studies have produced some very interesting facts regarding how the brain changes as the result of meditation.[2] Until the 1990s the belief was that the number of neurons in the brain was constant. It has now been proven that the brain generates new neurons when an action is repeated a great deal or if a person learns something new. For example, the part of the brain that gives instructions to the fingers becomes enlarged in concert pianists.

It has been known for some time that the brain activity of a depressed person shows a different pattern than that of a happy person. These brain states can be established with EEG (electroencephalogram) brain topology, a process of putting a large number of electrodes on the skull that measures the brain's activity, yielding a "brain map" of sorts. Through these studies, it has been found that happiness is associated with a high level of activity in the left frontal lobe (the part of the cerebral cortex lying directly behind the cortex), whereas a depressed person shows activity in the amygdala in the medial temporal lobes of the brain, which plays an important part in motivation and emotional behavior. The difference in activity in the left frontal lobe and the amygdala determines to a large extent whether the person is happy or a worrier.

The first experiment regarding meditation was carried out on a Tibetan monk who had done meditation exercises for more than 30 years. The center conducting the research compared the brain maps of 175 people who had never meditated to the brain map of the monk. The monk's prefrontal asymmetry score (that measuring activity in the frontal lobe) was higher than the highest score of any of the 175 other people tested. That was a promising start for the effects of meditation! The question arose, however, whether this monk might be a unique case.

The next experiment was carried out with employees of a biotech laboratory. These people were under considerable pressure to develop pharmaceutical drugs for commercial use. From that pool, only those people who were interested in learning more about meditation were enrolled in the study. All of these volunteers traveled to the University of Massachusetts, where their brains were measured with an EEG. Next, the group was split in two. Those in one half were told that they would have to wait for the meditation exercises, because the large number of applicants made it necessary to form two subgroups. This was not true, but was done to be able to compare the EEGs of the subgroup who had carried out the meditation exercises and the subgroup who had not.

The meditation program lasted ten weeks. One day every week a professional meditation teacher held two- to three-hour sessions and asked the participants to meditate every day for 45 minutes between the sessions. At the end of the ten-week program a one-day retreat was held. The EEG was again performed on those who had participated and on those on the waiting list. The meditation group showed a significant increase in activity in the left frontal lobe compared to the start of the meditation and compared with the group waiting for meditation training. The participants also reported that their anxiety level went down as well as their negative emotions.

The members of the meditation group as well those on the waiting list were given an influenza vaccine after the meditation program had finished. By taking a blood sample afterwards, it was possible to see whether meditation had any effect on the immune system. The analysis showed that the meditation group had a stronger immune response to the influenza vaccine. This was not a total surprise, as it was already known that high activity in the left frontal lobe predicts that a person's immune system will respond better to a vaccine, converting it into more antibodies against disease.

Further research at Harvard has found similar startling results:

An instructor at Harvard Medical School named Sara Lazar scanned the brains of 20 people who meditate for 40 minutes a day. These weren't Buddhist monks. Just regular people who had a long history of meditating. When she compared their brain images to those of nonmeditating people of similar ages and backgrounds, she found a highly significant difference. The meditators had 5% thicker brain tissue in the parts of the prefrontal cortex that are engaged during meditation – which is to say, the parts that handle emotion regulation, attention and working memory, all of which help control stress.[3]

START SIMPLE

I attended a 10-day meditation retreat in Thailand. The exercises consisted of both sitting and walking meditations combined with mindfulness training; or, rather, mindfulness training was integral to these two meditation forms. After three days of lectures, a one-week retreat started during which the only activities were walking and sitting. As a contrast to my daily life, I found it extraordinary not to talk to or even make eye contact with any of the participants for an entire week. I quickly learned, however, that it is this lack of external distraction that produces a kind of serene focus. I was taught to rotate the walking and sitting meditations throughout any given day. Since that time I have added the other meditation techniques and I practice almost every day. People tell me I have become calmer and more pleasant to deal with.

When you read about all these exercises you may become disheartened, as you cannot possibly do all of them at once. My recommendation is to start with the simplest exercises and spend just a few minutes a day on them. If you like the experience, gradually increase the time and add exercises. When you arrive at a point when you want to make more rapid progress, consider spending a week in a retreat, as Laurens did.

SIMPLE TECHNIQUES FOR BUSY LEADERS

Walking meditation

Walking meditation may be the simplest form of meditation to try, particularly for fast-moving Westerners. Its purpose is to develop mindfulness and concentration. "Mindfulness" refers to the ability to observe when emotions and thoughts become active in the brain. For example, when you are criticized you will notice that instead of listening intently, you start thinking, "This is unpleasant, I must defend myself, I do not like this person." In addition to noticing when a thought or emotion starts, mindfulness means that you develop the capability to "drop" the emotion or stop the thought. This must be done peacefully, not by trying to suppress it. The instruction is, "Note and drop."

Walking meditation is meditation in action. When we perform walking meditation, we are using the physical act of our bodies to bring us into greater awareness. It is the act of moving one foot in front of another that becomes our sole focus.

The correct way of walking is to walk evenly and naturally. Walk with your body *and* your mind. In other words, when your body is walking, let your mind be aware of the walking too, rather than allowing the ordinary path of the mind, which is to dwell on a problem or a thought. When your body is walking, your mind should not be thinking about the past or the future. If you feel your mind start to wander, bring it back to the physical act of walking, feeling the rhythmic nature of your steps. Let there be mindfulness, clear awareness of, and complete attentiveness to your walking body. Once you have found a rhythm, follow these key ways to take note of your body and mind:

❖ *Noting your body*. This is done by focusing your attention on your feet, such as walking very slowly and noting the movement and placement of the feet. Train your mind to be aware of the steps – left, right, left, right, and so on – and continually remind yourself to keep your attention there.
❖ *Noting your mind*. Be aware of the activity of your mind. When an emotion or a thought emerges, note if it is pleasant, unpleasant, or neutral, but do not attach any sentiment to that thought. Let it go and bring your attention back to your physical movements.

Walking meditation is an excellent way of developing our ability to bring awareness into our ordinary lives. For most of us, it is the easiest method of cultivating mindfulness and it can be incorporated into everyday life without much disruption. I urge everyone to try this method of meditation first, mostly because it does not require much behavioral change; you can practice it incrementally throughout the day as you go about your business.

A Western breathing technique

Many people know that if you get worried or stressed, taking deep breaths can be an effective way of calming down. The simple act of breathing is also an effective meditation technique. Its purpose is to calm the mind.

We think of breathing as an effortless act and thus don't give it much thought. But the way we breathe tells all: It is a reflection of our emotions and our ability to handle stress. Do you hold your breath when under pressure? Do you catch your breath when you need to make a decision quickly and the stakes are high? Or do you even know what happens to your breathing as you experience the ups and downs of life?

Many people are not aware of their breathing patterns. In Buddhism, we consider breathing to be a connection with a vital life force. If we use it properly, its natural rhythm can lead to a feeling of calm, and we know how valuable that state is. The next time you find yourself in a trying situation, take note of how you are breathing. Notice the tempo and rhythm and whether your breath seems strained. If it does, follow a simple pattern of controlling your breathing so that it falls into a slow, natural rhythm once again. As you breathe in fill up your belly and lungs, and as you exhale press out the air so that your belly contracts. Surprisingly, many people have been taught to breathe in exactly the opposite manner!

There are two effective ways for beginners to observe and control their breathing:

❖ *Counting.* You can choose to count to 4 or 6 on the inhale and the same measure on the exhale, making sure to keep a natural rhythm to your breathing. By counting, you are in essence also performing a mantra or meditation, which takes your mind off other worries.
❖ *Following.* Once your breathing takes on a natural rhythm, you can move beyond counting and simply follow the pattern – in, out, in, out. If you do this for five minutes, you immediately notice that your stress level reduces and your mind develops a much-needed clarity.

Sitting meditation

The purpose of sitting meditation is the same as for walking meditation, with the concentration on the breath instead of on the movement of the feet. With sitting meditation, we are more inclined to turn off external distractions and to focus on the process of meditating.

Sit cross-legged on the floor or instead choose a firm chair. What is important is to make sure that your back is straight and that you are not leaning on anything, which would give rise to excessive comfort and lead to sleepiness. It does not matter which posture you use; what is important is that your sitting position is comfortable and stable. A straight, unsupported back allows you to sit comfortably for a long period without putting great effort into balancing yourself. This is to prevent you worrying about your body, because the development of the mind through calm and insightful meditation is a subtle process.

Breathe in deeply and breathe out with a slow and long breath. Again breathe in deeply, fully, stretch your body, and breathe out with a slow and long breath. Do this 24 times and then breathe normally. Be aware of your sitting body; be aware of the exhalation and the inhalation. If your mind wanders to other thoughts, then as soon as you are aware of the thought, drop it and return to being mindful of your breath.

Sitting meditation requires just a bit more preparation than walking meditation, but for that reason it can also yield more profound results.

My experience with this exercise in the beginning was that it was more difficult than walking meditation. I found it easier to concentrate on the movement of the feet than on the breath, which is a required component of sitting meditation. The objective is the same as with walking meditation – to gain control over the emergence of thoughts and emotions – but the passivity and stillness required of sitting meditation (not to mention the cross-legged position!) are more physically challenging.

Both walking and sitting meditation will help you gain better control over negative emotions, reduce the amount your mind wanders, and improve concentration. But these results won't come immediately, or even after the first few sessions. As with all forms of meditation, consistent practice is the key.

One-pointed meditation

One-pointed meditation is, as the name implies, bringing your mind into focus by concentrating on a single object: a flower, a color, a pen, or a pebble. Some practitioners find it better to visualize the object with their eyes closed, whereas for others it is more effective to perform the meditation with their eyes open.

When your mind is focused on the object, it should be relaxed. However, if it is too relaxed there is a danger of your thoughts wandering or of sleepiness. You should have a certain degree of intensity, while maintaining single-pointedness, as though your mind has fused with the chosen object. This unusual combination of intensity and relaxed alertness is essential. The image should both be clear and stable.

Anant Asavabhokin, CEO of Land and Houses Ltd in Thailand, explained to me that he chooses a beautiful image of a mountain, the sea, or a landscape and concentrates on that.

At the end of a two-week session with the Dalai Lama, His Holiness presented me with a wonderful statue of Buddha that I have on my desk. When I do one-pointed meditation I try to remember the statue in minute detail. According to Buddhist instructions you should try to see the object in your mind as vividly and luminously as possible. That for me has been quite difficult, but when I succeed I feel peace afterwards.

Analytical meditation

The purpose of analytical meditation is to strengthen your ability to analyze a subject from many different perspectives and to concentrate on this subject for as long as you want. In analytical meditation you use reasoning skills[4] and bring about inner change through systematic investigation and analysis. In this way you can properly use your human intelligence – your capacity for reason and analysis – to contribute to your level of understanding and satisfaction with life. I should point out that the difference between one-pointed and analytical meditation is not the type of subject or object. The difference lies in how your mind is directed.

Take, for example, a negative emotion such as anger. You begin by reflecting on the destructive effects of anger on your physical health and emotional relationships. You should analyze this and reflect on it not just once or twice but repeatedly, until it becomes part of your deeper understanding. With this deeper understanding, now suppose someone harms you. Your immediate response is to become angry. When the emotion of anger arises you remember from your meditation the destructive nature of anger, and that immediately makes you more conscious of the undesirability of giving in to anger and letting it escalate within you, and in the process losing control over your mind.

This doesn't mean you shouldn't try to do something when someone attempts to harm you. On the contrary, you should take countermeasures to prevent harm to yourself and others — even strong countermeasures. But using this kind of meditation can help diffuse the intensity of your anger, which can have destructive effects, and you can instead respond to the situation without feeling hatred.

You may have committed harmful acts in the past that you regret, but these do not necessarily make you a permanently bad person. You can learn to separate another person's harmful actions from that person as a totality. Remind yourself that perhaps there are other factors at play that you are not aware of, which may have caused the person to act in the way they did. With practice, you can also analyze the situation from a wider perspective and even try to discover if this harmful act or difficult situation might be used in some way to enhance your spiritual growth, taken as an opportunity to make you stronger.

Another example of analytical meditation is developing appreciation of the efforts and kindness of others. Meditating on the value of kindness is a worthy effort. Our survival depends entirely on others. Having food depends on others; acquiring clothing depends on others; and obtaining housing depends on others. You may think "I paid for all these things," but that money did not come out of thin air; it depended on others. Then you may feel, "Yes, these are facts, but the others did not deliberately help me. They did it as a by-product of their efforts to survive." That is true. But I cherish many things that do not return my concern. For example, if my watch fell on the floor and broke, I would feel a loss. That does not mean that this watch has some feeling for me. It is useful to me, so I care about it. In the same way, all those people may not have done anything for us deliberately, but as their work is useful for us we should recognize their contribution. We depend on their contribution and their efforts for our own survival. Thinking along these lines will change your attitude.

Analytical meditation can therefore be applied to any concept of which you are trying to gain a better understanding. For example, if you wanted to develop a deeper comprehension of a difficult concept like "impermanence," you would make it the focus of your meditation and examine the concept as it applies to living things, dead things, and both short-term and long-term aspects of life. You would consider it in relation to different phenomena within the worlds of science, music, business, even happiness.[5] After such an examination your knowledge becomes more profound.

Visualization exercises

Visualization exercises involve some more advanced control over the mind. This type of meditation asks you to imagine yourself changing into something else, and its purpose for non-Buddhists is to calm the mind. Here is just one example of how to go about it.[6]

Imagine that you have three channels in your body. The central channel is a transparent tube about the width of your little finger, running straight down the center of your body from the crown of your head to the base of your spine.

The right and the left channels are also transparent tubes but are narrower than the central channel. They run from your nostrils up to the crown of your head, where they curve down like an umbrella handle to run along the central channel, parallel with the spine to slightly below your navel, where they join the central channel.

Having visualized these three channels, first breathe in through your left nostril, imagining that the air is flowing into the crown of your head and continuing down the left channel to the level of your navel, where it switches to the right channel. Here, you breathe out through that channel, passing the crown of the head and flowing out past the right nostril. Repeat this three times. Next, do the same exercise starting with the air coming in through the right nostril and going out though the left nostril. Do this three times. Lastly, breathe in through both nostrils together, bringing the air past the crown and down through the right and left channels to the point where they join the central channel. When the air reaches the central channel, tighten your inner pelvis and hold your breath. As soon as you no longer feel comfortable, exhale naturally through your nostrils, but visualize that, instead of the air going out, it dissolves inside the central channel. Do this three times.

When I read how to do this exercise for the first time, my reaction was that it was absolute nonsense. Being skeptical by nature, it took me some time to come around to attempting it.

The Buddha teaches that you should not believe anything until you have experienced it yourself and have made extensive verification based on your own experience. One of the most helpful descriptions of this attitude is presented by Piet Hut in his article "Life as a Laboratory."[7] An astrophysicist and professor at Princeton University, Hut writes:

After decades during which it was extremely unpopular among scientists to even mention the word "religion" I have seen many colleagues coming "out of the closet," as I have myself, by attending meetings and writing papers on the general topic of science and deeply felt human experience, with a nod to spirituality. I have started to view life as a laboratory, as an opportunity to examine ourselves and our world.

I found that Hut's view really hit home and I decided to give visualization a try. When I returned home from India after living for two weeks in a tent with very rudimentary facilities, my family expected me to be in bad shape. To their surprise I was perhaps a little thinner but in excellent spirits. The meditation had the desired effect; it certainly calmed my mind.

Citing mantras

Citing mantras is considered a more advanced form of meditation and does not come naturally to some people. Its purpose for non-Buddhists is again to calm the mind. The roots of the word mantra are "manna," which means mind, and "tra," which means protection.[8] Buddhists believe that citing a mantra, a sequence of words, can help to protect the mind from negative thoughts and emotions. We also believe that it is good for spiritual development.

Many different mantras exist for different purposes. For instance, when someone is focusing on developing a good heart, they concentrate on the mantra *Om Mani*

Padme Hum. This mantra is also often recited as a dedication when someone has died. When my mother passed away, my brother and I and many others recited *Om Mani Padme Hum* more than a hundred thousand times.

The meaning of *Om Mani Padme Hum* is very inspiring.[9] OM, pronounced as AUM or OHM, means body, speech, and mind. When we use the sound OM, it signifies that we would like to develop a pure body, speech, and mind, such as those of Buddha. Purity, here, refers to the absence of negative thoughts and emotions and of bad (unwholesome) actions. The remaining syllables indicate how to make this transition and use objects as symbols. MANI, meaning jewel, relates to Right Conduct, taking the right action inspired by an altruistic intention. PADME means lotus. A lotus is perfectly white even though it grows out of mud. It presents an image of your mind that is impure (stained with mud) and can become pure (white lotus flower), so relating to Right View. HUM means "indivisible"; that is, Right View and Right Conduct must be combined (see Chapters One and Two).

PART II

LEADING YOUR ORGANIZATION

*It is the task of the leader to create a company
with a strong and warm heart
and to see things as they really are*

CHAPTER FOUR

THE LEADER'S
PURPOSE

I AM THE HEAD of the Tibetan government-in-exile and Tibetans all over the world always give me a very hearty welcome. I see one of my most important tasks as giving Tibetans faith in the future. I am surprised how strong that faith is. Even though many live in miserable circumstances outside Tibet, they have remained a faithful and cheerful people.

A leader who inspires faith has to be very careful about engendering the right kind of faith. He or she should be honest and not demand blind faith. In the Buddhist tradition, we think that it is essential to combine faith with wisdom. Wisdom in this context means Right View, which we know means seeing the way things really are and understanding impermanence, interdependence, and dependent origination. Faith needs support – and this support comes from wisdom.

The wise leader examines the cause and effect of an objective or event, whether it is correct, appropriate, true, or false. If faith stands alone by itself, it is prone to deception and errors of judgment, and is easily influenced by emotion. Without wisdom we may believe whatever people tell us, no matter whether what they say is right or wrong. Faith may give us strength to do anything, even something evil. When faith is so strong, I remind people to keep it under the control of wisdom so as to stay in proper balance.

On the other hand, wisdom without faith is no good either because it lacks the strength to act. Wisdom supports faith by guiding it in a steady direction and sustaining it with perseverance. These two partners work together to reach the goal. Of course, in the end faith is a matter for the individual.

Many people feel that we do not have the right leaders, either in business or in government, and we certainly have many bad leaders. The resulting business scandals lead to businesses as a group having a poor reputation. Inadequate leadership at the level of countries results in poverty and war.

One significant problem is that people feel a lack of fairness. In prosperous countries this comes about as a consequence of an increase in inequality and growing insecurity about jobs; and in developing and poor countries people are conscious of social injustice to an unprecedented degree and resentful of their deprivation and lack of personal dignity. They hold their leaders responsible, both corporate and national.

Another major challenge is that leaders must be able to deal with crises. Increasing interdependence has two opposite effects: the system can deal more effectively with some shocks, but a small shock in one part can have disastrous consequences in others. One example can be seen in the fallout from the problems in the US subprime mortgage market at the end of 2007. The fact that lenders sold loans to people who could not afford them, and the subsequent packaging of those mortgages into various investment vehicles that later became nearly worthless due to the high level of foreclosures, led to losses estimated to be at least US$200 billion in major financial institutions worldwide. Given the interdependence of complex systems such as this, a leader must have the ability to maintain a calm, collected, and concentrated mind in a crisis.

The challenges are growing in importance and urgency. To meet them, leaders have to improve the performance of their minds. Following Right View and Right Conduct can make an important contribution in this. For example, if the people inside the company feel that they are respected and appreciated, that hiring and promotion practices are based on merit without any discrimination, they will perceive the company as fair. The same applies to customers, if organizations demonstrate a genuine interest in their wellbeing and if their business practices are shown to be equitable.

In this chapter we look at the necessity for a leader to establish a clear purpose for the company and to set values that should be observed by all. We also consider the traits a leader should develop, including effective decision making and coping with change, and suggestions for selecting and developing leaders.

DEFINING THE PURPOSE OF THE ORGANIZATION

Chester Barnard wrote a classic book about the tasks of the leader,[1] and his characterization still stands. He saw the leader's job as formulating and defining purpose; providing a system of communication; and attracting and retaining very competent people, encouraging them to put their best efforts into realizing the purpose of the business.

That sounds straightforward enough. So why is it that true leadership eludes so many? Because effective leadership requires the ability to build faith – and not everyone has that gift. Barnard comments:

Leadership must inspire cooperative decision making by creating faith: faith in the common understanding, faith in the probability of ultimate success, faith in the ultimate satisfaction of personal motives, faith in the integrity of the leadership, faith in the superiority of the common purpose of the organization as a personal aim of its members. Without the creation of faith, the catalyst by which the living system of human efforts is enabled to continue its incessant interchanges of energy and satisfactions, vitality will be lacking and the company will die. Cooperation, not leadership is the creative process; but leadership is the indispensable condition for its success.

The other essential element of good leadership is having an ability to clarify the organization's purpose, often a remarkably difficult task. Without a meaningful and achievable purpose, however, it is nigh-on impossible to attain a high level of morale and the right motivation in a company. People like – in fact they need – to know the purpose of what they are doing.

The importance of having a clear purpose was described very effectively by Jim Collins in his bestseller *From Good to Great*.[2] Collins compares "great" companies with others in the same industrial sectors: Great companies were defined by having much better performance (measured in shareholder value) over a period of 15 years. He found that it often took even great companies more than a year to define their purpose and several years to implement it. In fact, in most cases a competent top management team had to be fully in place before a purpose could be effectively enacted. Without leaders who believe in purpose, communicate it, act as an example, and make sure that employees work in accordance with the purpose, the concept falls flat.

In many companies the purpose is referred to as the "mission." Jack Welch, retired CEO of GE, recently found to his surprise that among those attending his seminars, 60% of CEOs did not have a company mission statement and 80% had no explicit set of company values. On top of that, he found that many mission statements were meaningless, like "Our mission is to be the best company in the industry," when compared to a useful statement such as that by Google, "To organize the world's information and make it universally accessible and useful."[3]

If you ask people what their purpose in life is, very few have a clear answer, though many people would wish for it. My answer to that question is very simple: the purpose of life is to be happy. And a shared purpose — a shared wish for happiness — is a precondition for people to identify with an organization. If they find out after joining the company that they do not like its purpose or that the company has no clear purpose, they will be disappointed and become unmotivated, and the chance for happiness will be lost. When people are clear about the purpose of a company, as communicated by strong leadership, joining the company will contribute to their happiness.

ESTABLISHING VALUES

In addition to clarifying an organization's purpose, one of a leader's main tasks and responsibilities is to define the values or principles that management and employees will adhere to when making decisions or taking action. Statements of such values go under many names, such as general business principles, values, codes of ethics, codes of conduct, or corporate responsibility statements.

Clearly, it is up to leaders to foster belief in this kind of statement and to act according to the principles. Because of this, the principles have to be established under the direct leadership of the chief executive, not delegated to anyone else.

Cor Herkströter, former CEO of Shell and at present Chairman of ING, reveals that these principles are immensely difficult to formulate. He comments that the value of principles increases enormously when they are "never" changed; principles that are changed from year to year become valueless to employees and in turn to the company. As he told me, "Once the principles have the right quality people will say, 'That's it, I could have written that myself.'"

Herkströter considers four characteristics of such principles to be essential:

❖ The principles should be clear and easy to understand.
❖ They should appeal to the people working for the company.
❖ They should help people to make responsible decisions.
❖ They must be meaningful in different cultures (for a global company).

An extension of the corporate code of conduct is the concept of "corporate citizenship," essentially the idea that a company must act as a responsible member of society, much as an individual citizen should. Many different names have been given to this rising movement: sustainable development, corporate social responsibility (CSR), and triple bottom line, to name but three.

No matter the term, one could say that that corporate citizenship is the application of the Buddhist concepts of Right View and Right Conduct to companies instead of to individuals. For instance, most companies when defining their values use the idea of "stakeholder." A stakeholder is not simply a financial investor, but when used in the context of corporate citizenship incorporates all the individuals and organizations affected by the actions of the company. That includes an inner circle of employees, shareholders, customers, and suppliers and many other organizations in the outer circle, such as NGOs, government bodies, and communities where the company operates. (The environment is also often included in this definition of stakeholder, as it is certainly affected by our actions.) Such a definition fits in well with the concept of Right Conduct.

The Dalai Lama explains the relevance.

Several of the business principles presented in statements of values and principles are examples of Right Conduct, for instance[4]:

❖ We expect all our employees to act with honesty, integrity, and fairness (*action*).
❖ We will help the people of the world to have fuller lives — both through the services we provide and through the impact we have on the world around us (*concern for the wellbeing of others*).
❖ We accept our responsibility to engage with communities and we will invest in society in a way that makes effective use of our resources, including support for charitable organizations (*responsible action*).
❖ We are committed to sustainable business practices and environmental protection (*concern for the environment*).
❖ Our customers have chosen to trust us. In return we must strive to anticipate and understand their needs and delight them with our service (*concern for the wellbeing of others*).

THE LEADER'S CHARACTER

So, the main tasks of a leader are clarifying purpose, defining values, building faith, and making the right decisions. And most people would agree that the quality of an organization's leadership is the greatest predictor of its success. But what kind of person is best suited to the job?

Chester Barnard distinguishes between "technical" skills and character:

A leader should have superior technical skills in understanding technology, in perception, in knowledge, in memory, in imagination. He should also have above average levels of determination, endurance, and courage.[5]

To lead in a Buddhist way one should build character through applying the principles of Right View and Right Conduct and then the desirable traits begin to form through consistent practice of these principles.

For example, an essential part of leadership is taking risks. If a decision turns out to be wrong, the leader is responsible. Someone appointed as a leader soon realizes that all the decisions about which there are strongly opposing views end up on his desk, so he or she requires courage.

When you follow the decision-making process of Right View and Right Conduct, decisions are analyzed from many perspectives, including their consequences for the company and for all its stakeholders. Thus the degree of risk is reduced, because you know you are making the right decisions.

At a highly successful company in the Netherlands, the chief executive and his top team went through the pros and cons of every important decision, sometimes getting involved in ferocious arguments. However, they didn't make any decisions until the following day, when the emotions had calmed down. Similarly, Nita Ing, Chief Executive of Continental Engineering in Taiwan, told me that she used to make decisions immediately because she wanted to be seen as a strong leader, but after practicing the concepts of Right View and Right Conduct she realized it was more important for decisions to be right than that they were taken quickly.

Buddhism proposes a useful list of the "seven character traits of an ideal person," which applies equally to leadership, as the Dalai Lama outlines.

Understanding principles and causes

Leaders are aware of what duties and responsibilities are involved in their role and of the challenges they face. Leaders should be able to identify the causes of problems and the principles that should be applied to solve them. For example, a problem can be caused by lack of self-discipline. If that is the case, the leader should know what steps to take to correct it.

Understanding objectives and results

Leaders know the meaning and objectives of the principles they abide by; they understand the tasks they are undertaking; they understand the reasons behind their actions. They know what may be expected in the future as a result of their actions and whether these will lead to a good or bad result. This kind of foresight is important for a leader when they are considering taking an action now that will only lead to results in the longer term, or are insisting on taking an action that is not popular.

Understanding oneself

Leaders know their strengths, knowledge, aptitudes, abilities, and virtues, and are able to correct and improve themselves. They also have to be aware of their limited knowledge of the operations of the company and how the company in turn affects its many stakeholder groups. They must be very eager to learn.

Understanding moderation

Leaders know moderation in speech, work, and action. They do everything with an understanding of the objectives and the real benefits expected. They do not act merely for their own satisfaction or to accomplish their own ends, but base their actions on the benefits for the organization for which they are responsible.

Understanding the occasion and efficient use of time

Leaders know the proper occasion and the proper amount of time for actions and dealings with other people — what should be done and how — and they do it punctually and at the appropriate time. This includes knowing how to plan one's time and organize it effectively. Additionally, leaders must have "discernment," the ability to identify the issues that matter most and concentrate on them. It is very important to avoid wasting time on trivial matters.

Understanding the organization

Leaders know that the organization should be approached this way: The people within it have rules and regulations; they have a culture and traditions; they have needs that should be dealt with, helped along, served, and benefited in the proper way. They need to have an understanding of the character of the company and their responsibility for developing that character, and they should be aware if some aspect of the character needs to be changed.

Understanding people
Leaders know and comprehend differences among individuals. They know how to relate to people effectively, what can be learned from them, how they should be praised, criticized, advised, and taught.

LEADERSHIP WITH A TRAINED MIND

Hundreds of books have been written about the characteristics of leaders and on how people can train themselves to become "great" leaders. All of these books present different prescriptions. The fact is that no two leaders are exactly alike, and it is also true that no one can become a great leader just by following a particular recipe. However, the Dalai Lama is convinced that if an individual with the right potential learns to think and act with a trained mind, his or her performance will greatly improve.

People who have never experienced the reality of being a leader often do not realize how demanding the job is. When I was promoted to president of the company for which I worked I was extremely happy. Soon thereafter I realized the difficulties, however: endless conflicts between people, a dissatisfied client, a company that could not pay, unfavorable currency fluctuations, good people who left, working 18 hours a day. The most difficult problems, those on which people cannot agree, always end up on the leader's desk. And that is the way it should be. Of course, there were also many happy moments, but being a leader is very hard work. A leader must develop the capability to cope with the inevitable ups and downs and maintain a calm, collected, and concentrated mind under all circumstances, however adverse.

Buddhist teachings contain innumerable lists on how to cope with different problems. We have selected one that is particularly relevant for leaders, the so-called Eight Worldly Concerns. These are about states or events that occur to all of us: criticism, praise, failure, success, making money, losing money, being famous, and not receiving any recognition whatsoever. The Dalai Lama offers a simple explanation of these concerns.

The Eight Worldly Concerns are presented in what appears to be a confusing and conflicting way, but this is deliberate. They consist of four pairs that appear to be contradictory:

❖ Becoming distressed when someone insults or belittles you.
❖ Becoming elated when someone praises you.

❖ Feeling depressed when you experience failure.
❖ Feeling happy when you experience success.

❖ Being dispirited when you become poor.
❖ Being joyful when you acquire wealth.

❖ Feeling upset when you lack recognition.
❖ Feeling pleased when you achieve fame.

The first concern, becoming distressed when someone belittles you, appears to be just as natural as becoming elated when someone praises you. But in fact, although it seems natural, it is the wrong reaction for someone with a trained mind. When a person with an untrained mind is belittled they become unhappy or angry. The person with a trained mind reacts differently. They ask themselves: "What is the motivation of the person who is belittling me? Is this person competent to hold an opinion? Is the opinion justified?" If it is justified, there is something to learn and one should explain that one unfortunately made a mistake. If the opinion is not justified, explain why. If the other person is acting out of malice, someone with a trained mind will see this as an opportunity to test their ability to stay calm without any negative emotions like anger. Their reaction should depend on what conclusion their reflection leads to.

The same process should be followed when being praised. What is the motivation of the person giving the praise? Is the praise being given from a person who understands what has been accomplished? Is their judgment valuable or do they want to please or, worse, flatter because they desire something in return? Praise and criticism have to be dispassionately evaluated for what they are worth. The right objective or motivation is not avoiding criticism or getting praise – the objective is to do the right thing.

The reasoning is the same with the other pairs. Feeling depressed when you experience failure is as natural as feeling happy when you experience success. However, I consider being depressed as a negative emotion; it does not have a positive value. Instead of increasing one's energy to solve a problem, it leaves one with less energy. Therefore, a person with a trained mind will analyze if the failure is due to mistakes or to external circumstances. If it is diagnosed as a mistake, can anything be learned to avoid similar failures in the future? Being elated by success does not have the negative consequence of reducing energy and instead increases positive energy. The danger lies in believing that the success was entirely due to your own brilliance, and that the success of all future actions is therefore certain. Every successful outcome is the result of many causes coming together. The decision the successful person took may have been only one of the causes. It is important to reflect on the contributions other people have made and the other circumstances that have made the success possible. And, of course, the idea that someone will be successful in everything they do is dangerous because it can lead to arrogance and false pride.

The third pair is also perfectly natural – being dispirited when you become poor and joyful when you acquire wealth. Nobody acts with the intention of becoming poor. Or in business terminology, no business intends to make a loss. But the reality is that many businesses occasionally do lose money. Becoming dispirited when that happens is of no use. The right frame of mind is to figure out how the losses can be changed into profits. Being dispirited is, again, a negative emotion. Being joyful when the company is successful, including making good profits, is natural. The risk is that it is seen as something permanent. Some years later, unless the right changes are made, the company will lose money. Therefore, being happy is fine as long as it does not lead to thinking that a company that does not change will remain successful.

Being pleased with fame can be the result of a person seeking fame. Fame is like wealth: It can easily lead to an insatiable desire for more. The first problem is that someone with an insatiable desire for fame will never be happy, as fame will always be limited. There will always be people who are more famous. The second point is that fame is only fine when it is the result of right action. It is bad when it is sought for its own sake without regard for the right actions. It requires considerable effort for an ambitious person not to become addicted to fame.

Clearly, there is a pattern here: celebrating joyful events while not becoming too attached to their meaning, either in the present or as a predictor of the future.

Examples of both criticism and success are plentiful in the workplace. One in particular comes to mind: A CEO of a leading software company learns that she has been selected as one of the best 100 managers of the year. She feels pleased, as well she should. (If she had been listed as one of the worst, she'd naturally be unhappy.) The managers who are not on the list think that they should have been selected and are jealous. (Others who were afraid they might be chosen as one of the worst are happy that they are not on the list.) These reactions are natural.

A person with a trained mind and Right View will think as follows: She will be pleased for being selected but will also reflect on the help she received from others – and that she has been lucky. A leader chosen as one of the worst leaders should first take time to calm down, because it is unavoidable that he will be unhappy. He realizes that the people in his company will read about it; his family and friends will also know. He realizes that getting angry and blaming others or the magazine is a waste of mental energy. The next step is to determine if there is any justification in his selection and if there are lessons to be learned. He should also share his thoughts with others. What can they do together to improve the situation? The essential insight of Right View is that we must learn to direct our mind in a constructive way, especially when our ego has been hurt.

Nita Ing, chief executive of Continental Engineering in Taiwan, told me about an important event in her life that came about as a result of the application of Right View. She is chairwoman of the Taiwan High-Speed Rail Corp (THSRC), which bid for the US$15 billion contract to build a high-speed train system in Taiwan. The consortium she was bidding against had close links to the government in power, while Nita Ing supported the head of the opposition party. When the bids were opened, THSRC's bid was substantially lower in price and higher in quality. It is not hard to imagine the government's dismay at having to award the largest contract in Taiwanese history to a consortium led by a woman supporting the opposition.

As might be expected, a campaign was launched to change the outcome. Tax inspectors were sent in to check Continental Engineering's accounts in an attempt to find illegal activity such as tax evasion. Nita Ing and her children were threatened. The media became heavily involved and she was made out to be incompetent to handle such a large contract. It all became too much for her to bear. An independently wealthy woman, she questioned why she should ruin her life and those of her children just to win a contract.

Nita Ing informed her Buddhism teacher that she was going to quit the following day. Her teacher, Zopa Rinpoche,[6] said, "You must do what you think is right, but think about the fact that the project you are involved in is a great gift."

Nita Ing's reaction was, "A gift? You cannot be serious – it is destroying me."

Her teacher answered, "It is a great gift because it gives you a great opportunity to achieve change for the better. Please do one thing for me, think about it. And calm down. Do not make a decision when you are upset because you do not see things the way they really are."

After some hesitation, Nita Ing decided to follow his advice. She thought about her decision overnight and did not quit – and her consortium won the contract.

DEVELOPING MINDFULNESS

Applying Right View and particularly mindfulness, as outlined in Chapters One and Three, helps you become aware of feelings, perception, and consciousness as they manifest themselves in your brain. Say a CEO has called a meeting of senior executives to discuss an important issue for which everyone's input is needed. The meeting is to start at 10 o'clock. When the CEO arrives at that time, he notices (*feeling*) that one of his executives is not there (*perception* and *consciousness*). He now has several options to choose from: waiting until the missing person arrives, starting the meeting anyway, calling the person on his mobile phone, or calling his secretary to find out why the person is not there. For the untrained person this process has an emotional dimension. The CEO feels annoyed that the executive has not shown up. He may see it as a lack of discipline or a lack of respect for him and for the other participants who have all come on time. He might well become angry, especially if the missing person is often late – a typical example of how negative thoughts and emotions arise.

These all seem like natural reactions, but recognize that people with an untrained mind often misinterpret the situation. In the cycle of feeling, perception, and consciousness, they instantly classify a feeling into categories: like, do not like, friendly, unfriendly, positive or negative, and so on.

On the flip side, the person with a trained mind learns how to avoid this instant classification. Making the right choice depends on seeing reality, the ability to generate constructive solutions, and taking decisions with a calm and collected mind. This Buddhist method consists of four steps:

1   What is the reality and is it a problem?
2   What is the cause of the problem?
3   What do I want to achieve?
4   How can I arrive at the goal?

Let's return to our example and consider a potential response after thinking it through in the right way. When the senior manager does not arrive on time to the meeting, the CEO will not get upset, angry, or worried. He will first find out the cause. Until he knows the cause he will not think about the action he may take. Once he does know why the manager was late, he will determine what he wants to accomplish.

Here a person with a trained mind will consider different perspectives. How important is it that everyone arrives on time to meetings? What are the consequences of the different actions he could take? What is the perspective of the missing person and of the others in the meeting? Might there be acceptable reasons for a person being late without notifying the CEO? Would an acceptable reason for being late be that the person was on the phone with one of the company's most important clients about a very significant contract?

If the CEO concludes that a late arrival to an important meeting is a serious problem, he will think about how he can change the behavior of people who are often late. So what will the CEO do? When the missing person arrives the CEO will summarize the discussions up to that point, underscoring the importance of the content and of being present to receive it. What he will not do is to show anger toward the senior manager who was late, because a person with a trained mind has learned that getting angry is unlikely to solve the problem. If he thinks it is a serious problem, he will raise it either with the person individually or in another meeting and present the results of his analysis.

The core belief behind distinguishing between feelings, perception, and consciousness is that you will be able to make better decisions. It is an example of developing mindfulness.

If an organization seeks out leaders who exhibit the qualities described in this book, it will be placing its trust in those who put the wellbeing of the organization as a whole above all other considerations. Many leaders in the modern-day corporate environment do not think this way. In fact, some think the opposite: They consider they should maintain distance from their employees, and be shrewd and heartless in the face of tough decision making. What leaders should in fact focus on is the need to satisfy employees, customers, and shareholders. This can be done through a variety of means, many of them financial, but it also requires maintaining a good reputation and a high level of motivation in the organization. Leaders who possess the characteristics described in this book will be able to meet these objectives by having a clear purpose and applying wisdom.

CONTINUITY OF LEADERSHIP

Given the vital role that a leader plays in a company, appointing the right person is one of the most important considerations. This is the responsibility of the board of directors. When looking for a successor to an incumbent chief executive, the best solution may be to appoint someone who is already working for the company. Such a person is already known by the board members, employees, and other stakeholders. The challenge for the company is to have a succession-planning system in place that identifies people with the potential to become leaders and to develop their competences and skills systematically.

Unfortunately the majority of companies do not have such a system. Why? It is a problem of lack of courage. Board members find it uncomfortable to talk to the current chief executive about who should replace him (or her) if he leaves. Most chief executives love their job and if they had the choice would postpone their retirement indefinitely. Therefore, many only show a lukewarm interest in succession planning.

Someone from outside the company carries a much higher risk when appointed to a CEO position and may well have to be paid much more than an insider. The importance of payment should not be underestimated. Many insiders are very keen to get such a job even with only a small increment over their current pay. An outsider may have to be paid double that amount. Apart from this increase for one person, doing so would pull up the compensation of other members of top management, so the total extra costs are far higher than just the increase in compensation for the outsider. Nevertheless, even in companies with a succession-planning system an outsider may have to be chosen if none of the internal candidates is suitable, and there may be circumstances when "fresh blood" is a benefit, particularly in times of change.

There are few decisions that the board takes that are more important than making sure that competent successors are selected as heads of companies. In this chapter we have described the characteristics they should be looking for. We have also indicated that these characteristics can be developed and should therefore be part of skills development for potential leaders.

After working on this book and realizing how complicated the role of a corporate leader is, I have become convinced that leaders need to develop a holistic view of business. In the past it may have been enough for a leader to concentrate on leading the people in his or her organization. This is no longer enough. A leader must also engage with governments, NGOs, customers, and shareholders. For this engagement to be effective, the leader must try to understand the very different ways of thinking of these other groups. Adversarial relationships are to be avoided, so in this context humility is very important. These other groups often understand very little about the world of business, and they may have many beliefs that do not correspond to reality. It is the task of the leader to help them find the "truth." An arrogant attitude will have negative consequences. Patience and respect for others are essential. The people appointing the successor should keep this in the back of their minds at all times: This person will be responsible for providing the company with a strong and warm heart. Can he or she do that?

My own succession is also of great concern to me. This is complicated, because a definite and final solution can only be established after the government in China recognizes and accepts that the establishment of Tibet as a genuine autonomous region within China is the only and best solution for China and for the Tibetans. My health is very good and I hope that this will happen still in my lifetime. But as a responsible leader I have to prepare for the eventuality that it will only happen after my death. The Right View is impermanence and therefore a change in the attitudes of the Chinese government is inevitable. While the Chinese government has already reduced restrictions on religious freedom since the 1980s, it is impossible to predict when the right attitude change concerning Tibet will occur.

Right action in this situation requires patience and skill. I have therefore decided to examine with the most senior members of the Tibetan community how to organize my succession, in case a change in attitude by the Chinese government comes too late. We will select the most capable man or woman, acceptable and fully supported by the Tibetan people and by the religious leaders in Tibetan Buddhism, to provide continuity of leadership after my death. That is my duty.

CHAPTER FIVE

CREATING PROFIT, JOBS – OR HAPPINESS?

ANY ORGANIZATION IS both more and less than the sum of its members. It is less because the members of the group devote only a part of their time to the organization; and more because the organization as a whole can accomplish tasks the individual members cannot succeed in carrying out on their own.

The other day, when I was traveling from the railway station in Pathankot to where I live in Dharamsala, the car was halted because woodsmen were cutting down a tree that was at risk of falling onto the road. After the tree was felled, two skinny old men started to saw the trunk into pieces so that the road could be cleared. As you can imagine, an ever-growing number of cars began to queue up on both sides of the tree. Many people got out of their cars to watch the two men struggling with their saw. There must have been more than 100 people watching the two men work. Then one of the spectators came forward and with a wave of his arm invited other people to join him in pushing the tree to the side of the road. In less than five minutes 20 men had moved the tree and the traffic obstruction was removed.

This so simply demonstrated what people can do when they cooperate. It also occurred to me that if nobody had taken the initiative to move the tree in a cooperative effort, we would have had to wait more than two hours before we could have continued. The people moving the tree were not a business, not even organized, but they had a common purpose and a spontaneous leader who took the initiative to solve the problem.

If part of the role of the leader is to clarify purpose and inspire faith in organizational goals and values, as outlined in Chapter Four, then what role does the organization play? Is the real purpose of business simply to make a profit – to "maximize shareholder value" – or is there is something larger at stake? Of course, business leaders will argue that profit is paramount, otherwise a company cannot survive. That is true, but more forward-thinking leaders recognize that aside from profit, businesses and organizations can achieve other admirable goals.

Decades ago, in 1977, professor Peter Drucker commented:

A business cannot be defined or explained in terms of profit. Asked what a business is, the typical businessman is likely to answer, "An organization to make profit." The typical economist is likely to give the same answer. This answer is not only false; it is irrelevant. The concept of profit maximization is, in fact, meaningless. Profitability is not the purpose of, but the limiting factor on, business enterprise. Profit is not the explanation, cause or rationale of business decisions, but a test of their validity. The purpose of a business must lie outside the business itself. In fact it must lie in society, since business enterprise is an organ of society.

Buddhist businessman Dhaldol Bumag, CEO of AIG-Thailand, offers an additional way to see the role of the organization:

For me the purpose of my business is to build a team of successful people with high morale, good attitudes and good faith. Building the agency force to sell insurance is to teach them to bring benefits to others. Profits are just an end result rather than the purpose of business.

And Buddhist scholar Venerable P. A. Payutto comments as follows:

From the Buddhist point of view, economic activity should be a means to a good and noble life. Production, consumption and other economic activities are not ends in themselves; they are means, and the end to which they must lead is the development of well-being within the individual, within society and within the environment.[1]

THE BUDDHIST VIEW OF PROFIT

In the Buddhist tradition we have a very clear view of profit. Profit is a fine aim, as long as it as been earned honestly. To state that the role of business is to make a profit makes as much sense as to say that the role of a person is to eat or to breathe. If a company loses money it dies, as does a person without food, but that does not mean that the purpose of life is eating.

My preference would be for businesses to define their role as "creating and satisfying customers" while acting responsibly, rather than "maximizing shareholder value" alone. Sure, acting responsibly includes making a healthy profit and delivering satisfactory increases in shareholder value. But the danger of making profit the single, most important objective creates conditions that are bound to lead to breaking the law and causing unnecessary suffering for a large number of people.

Certainly, employees do not want to work for a company that is losing money, for that imperils their job security. On the other hand, they want to work for a company of which they can be proud, a company that has a solid reputation as a supplier of high-quality, useful products and services. That is why defining the organization's role in a motivating and positive way is very important.

CREATING WEALTH

Wealth is obviously important for business and wealth can be an important force for good. It is the product of work, and in Buddhism work is considered to be very important. A person's first responsibility is to take care of themselves, and next to help others. Life is about acting with good intentions. A job provides excellent opportunities to act, because the results benefit ourselves and others.

The improper use of wealth
Wealth can also be used the wrong way. It can be used to harmful ends such as corruption. Buddhism also considers hoarding wealth as using it the wrong way. The following story illustrates this point.[2]

The Buddha was once visited by Pasenadi, King of Kosala. The king explained that a wealthy man who had just died had left no instructions regarding the disposal of his property. Therefore, Pasenadi had ordered that the goods be brought to the royal residence. Vast quantities arrived, gold and silver. Yet, the deceased had always dressed in very poor garments and had been in the habit of eating only sour husk-gruel. Since this man had not utilized his wealth properly, either on his own account or on that of his parents, wife, children, workers, or friends, it would be confiscated by the ruler or appropriated by heirs for whom he had no regard.

The Buddha confirmed that this would have been the natural order of events, and that in the opposite circumstances, if the wealthy man had allocated his wealth properly, he would have been happier himself, would have made others happy, and his charitable deeds and almsgiving would have left a happy memory. His riches would not have been wasted. Both the squandering and the hoarding of wealth are therefore deplored.

In Buddhism, we think a great deal about death, the importance of accepting death as an inevitable fact, and the desirability of dying satisfied with what one has done. In the above story, it is almost certain that the person died alone without anybody at his side and suffered because he had to abandon his wealth.

Becoming wealthy in the right way
Buddha taught that becoming wealthy in the right way was as important as using earned wealth in the proper way. This is well illustrated by the following quote from Buddha:

Good and praiseworthy people are those who seek wealth in rightful ways and use it for the good and happiness of both themselves and others.

A parable ascribed to Buddha describes this concept in further detail:

Monks, there are three groups of people in this world. What are these three? They are the blind, the one-eyed, and the two-eyed.

Who is the blind person? There are some in this world who do not have the vision that leads to the acquisition of wealth or to the increase of wealth already gained. Moreover, they do not have the vision that enables them to know what actions lead to positive results, and the ones that do not, they do not know what deserves disapproval, what is vulgar, and what is refined, good and evil. That is what I mean by the one that is blind.

Who is the one-eyed person? These people have the vision to acquire wealth but are otherwise the same as the blind person. This I call a one-eyed person. And who is the two-eyed person? These people have the vision to acquire wealth and capitalize on it, have the vision that enables them to know what actions lead to positive results, and the ones that do not, what deserves disapproval and what not, what is vulgar and what is refined, good and evil. This I call the person with two eyes.

The one who is blind is hounded by misfortune on two counts: he has no wealth, and he performs no good works.

The second kind of person, the one-eyed, looks about for wealth irrespective of whether it is right or wrong. It may be obtained through theft, cheating or fraud. He enjoys pleasures of the senses from his ability to acquire wealth. The one-eyed person suffers according to his deeds.

The two-eyed person is a fine human being, one who shares out a portion of the wealth obtained through his diligent labor. He has noble thoughts, a resolute mind and will be free of suffering. Avoid the blind and the one-eyed, and associate with the two-eyed.[3]

This parable is very relevant for businesspeople. Leaders must have vision to be able to succeed in creating wealth, and also know what kind of action to take so that the vision will be realized. They should also know what kind of action is wrong or disreputable and distinguish between actions that are good and bad. Furthermore, good businesspeople share a portion of their gains with others. This sharing with others is a fundamental aspect of the Buddhist view of wealth. The story also says in a roundabout way that a good businessperson will be happy: "He… will be free from suffering."

"The one-eyed person… enjoys pleasures of the senses from his ability to acquire wealth" can be misunderstood without an explanation. "Enjoying the senses" in Buddhist texts can have two meanings, positive and negative. For example, there is nothing wrong with enjoying a good meal. But the parable refers to a person who is vulgar and does not know what is refined. He may therefore become addicted to good food, eat too much, and grow obese. He may be unhappy when he has to eat a simple but healthy meal. There are many other such addictions like gambling, drinking too much, and so on.

"The one-eyed person suffers according to his deeds" refers to the Buddhist belief that a person who acts badly will suffer. I realize that most Westerners believe that even though some people act badly, in doing so they become rich and enjoy a luxurious and happy life. Buddhists do not think that this is possible. Bad actions will catch up with a person sooner or later. There is no scientific proof of whose view is right. Personally, I believe that businesspeople who earn their wealth honestly and share some of it with others will be happier than those who cheat or behave like the one-eyed man.

The proper use of wealth

Buddha presented the same ideas in another way, in the form of a "check list," with eight questions leaders can ask themselves if they want to know if they are using their wealth in proper ways. The "best" answer is indicated in brackets after each question.

❖ Did you acquire wealth lawfully? *(Yes, I did)*
❖ Did your wealth provide happiness only to you? *(No, also to others)*
❖ Did your wealth provide happiness also to others? *(Yes, it did)*
❖ Did you share your wealth with others? *(Yes, I did)*
❖ Did you carry out any good deeds with your wealth? *(Yes, I did)*

A "good deed" involves making others happy or relieving suffering.

❖ Are you attached to and infatuated by your wealth? *(No, I am not)*

"Attached to" means that someone has become stingy and mean. "Infatuated" means that they think they are very important, deserve to be respected, and know the right answer to every question, because they are wealthy.

❖ Are you heedful of the dangers of wealth? *(Yes, I am)*

"Heedful" is an important concept in Buddhism. It means that someone is aware of what is going on in their mind. They will recognize when their mind becomes infatuated or mean or stingy and will stop the "becoming" process in its tracks.

❖ Do you possess the insight that leads to spiritual freedom? *(Yes, I do)*

"Insight that leads to spiritual freedom" refers to understanding that wealth can increase and decrease for reasons a person cannot control. There is nothing wrong with being happy when wealth increases, but it is wrong to become unhappy when it decreases. If someone becomes overly attached to their wealth, he loses his spiritual freedom and becomes worried about anything that would reduce his wealth.

Businesspeople can grade themselves using this list. The highest level is reached by those who seek wealth lawfully, and in so doing provide happiness for themselves and others. They share their wealth and perform good deeds; moreover, they are not attached to or infatuated with their wealth, they are heedful of its dangers, and they possess the insight that leads to spiritual freedom.

Buddha never praised or advocated poverty. He thought at an early stage in his life that he could become happy by living in a forest and starving himself close to death. He found that this did not work and concluded that it was not the right way. That is why he recommended that monks and nuns should lead a modest but comfortable life. He saw poverty as the cause of immorality and crime. Buddha suggested that in order to eradicate crime, people's economic condition should be improved. Grain (for sowing) and other facilities for agriculture should be provided to farmers and cultivators. In a crisis capital should be provided for traders and those engaged in business. Adequate wages should be paid to those who are employed. When people are provided for, earning sufficient income, they will be content, will have no fear or anxiety, and consequently the country will be peaceful and free from crime.[4]

A LIVING ENTITY

Organizational development specialist Peter Senge points out another reason why looking at a business as a moneymaking machine is erroneous: A machine wears out, whereas a business can renew itself; it may become obsolete, but that is because of poor performance by its employees or market conditions.[5] A machine cannot be motivated; it does what it is programmed to do. Members of an organization, however, do need to be motivated to realize the purpose of the business. A machine is not conscious and does not have a conscience, whereas an organization can be seen to have a shared consciousness and a shared conscience. It is thus much more appropriate to look at a business as a living entity than as a machine.

Organizational learning consultant Arie de Geus expands on this:

All companies exhibit the behaviour and certain characteristics of living entities. All companies learn. All companies, whether explicitly or not, have an identity that determines their coherence. All companies build relationships with other entities, and all companies grow and develop until they die… Like all organisms, the living company exists primarily for its own survival and improvement: to fulfil its potential and to become as great as it can be.[6]

It is an interesting question whether a business has a conscience, in the sense of knowing what is right and wrong. All people have a conscience, but the sense of what is right and wrong varies enormously between individuals. It is the same for businesses, but it is more complicated. A company's network of consciousness includes many people with different ideas of what is right and wrong. Experience shows that people in business will do things they would not do in their private lives. That proves that business as a whole influences the conscience of individuals when working for a company. This influence can make people act better or worse than they would on their own. Unfortunately, the influence of business on the moral standards of the individual can be negative, especially when business leaders put pressure on employees to produce profits, without emphasizing the overriding importance of those profits being honestly gained and based on Right Conduct and Right View.

A human being has a physical body that includes a brain, a consciousness, and a conscience. A business is not such an integrated system. Offices, equipment, machines, inventories, shops, computers, and so on are not like a body. They have no sensors that are online to the brain. These physical things are only of value in their relationship to the people that use them, and then only as those people relate to each other in a network between the employees, their customers, and suppliers.

Nevertheless, this difference is not as large as you may think. What is a person without a network of relationships with family, friends, and acquaintances? A person only truly "exists" through relationships with others. Therefore, a business consists of an invisible network of relations between people. The true value of a business is not the sum of its facilities and its employees and its financial resources: The value resides in the relationships between the people within it and with the many stakeholders outside the organization.

BUSINESS AND HAPPINESS

Businesses are normally not seen as producers of happiness. A company leader that described one of his or her goals as to produce happiness would risk ridicule. When I started on this project I was not sure to what extent businesses would be able and willing to see creating happiness as one of their goals, but I now see that is a real possibility, particularly if we see happiness in terms of "satisfaction with life."

I believe that the desire of people to be happy and avoid suffering is universal. At the superficial level there may be many differences. Cultures have different habits and traditions. Therefore some actions will create offense in one country but not in another. But fundamentally nobody wants to be poor without shelter or sufficient food, not having the means to send children to school, being without friends, not being respected by others, not having the freedom to express an opinion. The vast majority of people in all cultures agree with the goals in the United Nations Declaration of Human Rights, such as "Everyone has the right to life, liberty and security of person" and "All human beings are born free and equal in dignity and rights. They are endowed with reason and conscience and should act towards one another in a spirit of brotherhood."[7]

If the role of each individual within the organization in achieving its purpose is recognized – better yet, celebrated on a regular basis – workers find greater meaning in their work, their organization, and their life.

Leaders have an enormous influence on the wellbeing of their employees beyond providing a job and paying a salary. Many employee satisfaction studies conclude that "trust" is one of the most important factors here. Employees want to feel that they are trusted by management and that they can trust management in return. Related to trust is that people want to feel they have enough freedom to perform a good job. If they have no freedom and everything they do is inspected and controlled, employees quickly become unhappy. They perceive this as a lack of trust, but also as a lack of respect.

One way for leaders to improve job satisfaction is to show respect for their people by investing in training and development. People not only appreciate being trained in the necessary skills for doing their job, they also notice when an employer shows interest in their stress levels and overall health. Employees also enjoy participating in social events as a group and these events often rank high on employee satisfaction polls. Furthermore, people like to be informed how the business is doing and what the future looks like. If the news is good, it provides a sense of ease among staff; if the news is bad but is still delivered candidly, it can encourage fresh cooperation to solve the problem.

Since unemployment can lead to suffering in the form of hunger, poverty, and losing the respect of others, the hope is that leaders will recognize these consequences before taking action solely with shareholders in mind. Jobs provide income and income provides freedom: freedom to pay for shelter, food, healthcare, and education. Jobs also provide self-respect and the possibility to make progress materially and spiritually. To deprive people of these basic needs without great consideration can create significant unhappiness.

The Maslow model

Psychologist Abraham Maslow developed the concept that happiness depended on satisfying different needs, and that

some fundamental needs had to be satisfied before others could be considered.[8] This is referred to as the "hierarchy of needs" and the concept is often presented as a pyramid with five levels.

Maslow claimed that people had to satisfy the lower-level needs before being able to move to the next level up. The basic needs of food, water, and shelter fall into the lower categories and income plays a role in satisfying these needs. People at low levels of income may only be able to focus on the basic needs and thus are often satisfied with taking almost any job that provides food, water, shelter, etc. When those needs are satisfied, people are no longer happy with just any job: They want an interesting job that contributes to their higher-level needs, as they eventually move up to level 5, "self-actualization." Someone reaches that stage if they feel that all their talents and capabilities are being used in a satisfactory way.

Having a job is important at all levels. It provides income to buy food at level 1 and the stability of level 2. A company is a kind of community with personal relationships; they may be not affectionate, but most people establish friendships with some of their colleagues at work (level 3). A job gives self-respect and independence at level 4. Many people in prosperous countries are at level 5, and there they realize self-actualization.

Maslow's theory reminds me of the Alavi story.[9] Buddha arranged a meeting with Alavi to give him some teaching. Buddha walked for miles and was warmly welcomed by the inhabitants of the town where the peasant lived, but Alavi himself was not there. One of his cows had escaped and it took a lot of effort on his part to find the cow. When the peasant arrived at the place set up for the talk, he was exhausted and very hungry. When Buddha saw Alavi's condition, he asked the city elders to arrange some food for the poor man, and only when the peasant had eaten his fill and was refreshed did the Buddha start to teach. The Buddha afterwards explained his reasons: "When people are overwhelmed and in pain through suffering, they are incapable of understanding religious teaching."

This story illustrates the hierarchy of needs. The level 1 needs, the physiological needs, first have to be satisfied before the higher levels can be activated.

Happiness in the Maslow model is based on the assumption that the needs at all five levels can be satisfied. In contrast, according to the Buddhist way of thinking, it is impossible ever to satisfy all these needs. To a Buddhist the objective is also happiness, but in the sense of "peace of mind" not of "satisfying all needs." By training the mind to avoid thoughts and actions that lead to suffering, and also to cope with adverse events that will inevitably happen like old age, loss of family members, or loss of wealth, happiness or "acceptance" can be achieved.

The basis of Maslow's theory is to satisfy the needs of the individual, of the self. According to Buddhist thinking, in contrast, there is no independent, permanent, unchanging self. The self consists of relationships with other people and other aspects of the physical environment. All people, not least in Western society, are obsessed by the "self": "This is mine," "I am being offended," "I do not make enough money," or "People are not nice to me." In the Buddhist concept, it is not other people who have to satisfy the needs of an individual, it is the reverse. People can only be happy if they satisfy the needs of other people as well as their own.

Money can't buy happiness

A wealth of data in recent decades has shown that once the personal needs of food, shelter, and basic comfort have been met, increased wealth has little bearing on happiness. In other words, "money can't buy happiness." Rather than moving up the Maslow pyramid away from basic needs, people in industrialized nations may become more consumerist but not seek out a greater sense of belonging or activities that lean toward self-actualization, and so happiness eludes them. They are obsessed with wealth and focus on unwholesome rather than wholesome consumption. Unwholesome consumption uses goods and services merely to satisfy desires and for ego gratification. Wholesome consumption contributes to the wellbeing of people and takes care of basic needs.

One important factor is "keeping up with the Joneses." Most people like to maintain the same standard of living as others who they consider belong to the same group. If a neighbor switches to a flat-panel television, they want to do the same. If they cannot afford this, it has a negative influence on their happiness. Equally, though, if they can afford it, they run up against economist Fred Hirsch's concept of "positional goods," which have a value in relation to their high status or scarcity. If everyone had a Ferrari, for example, it would no longer hold the same cachet as a possession. Happiness in this consumer context is therefore never attainable.[10]

There is an increasing amount of research into what happiness is and how it can be measured, ranging from that by economists such as Richard Layard and Andrew Oswald to that by psychologists such as Ed Diener and Martin Seligman.[11] More than 1,700 studies have been conducted into happiness and wealth in over 40 countries, for example.[12]

One of the most prominent studies is that carried out by Professor Ruut Veenhoven at Erasmus University, who maintains the World Database of Happiness.[13] The data shows that when people are poor, their happiness on average rises with their income. If income is above a certain level, happiness stays constant. One's income level is important, but the direction of change is significant too. When income is increasing people are obviously much happier than when it is declining. Someone with a higher income that is declining is less happy than someone with a lower income that is increasing.

Nevertheless, money is not the only factor. Bruno Frey and Alois Stutzer, two prominent Swiss economists, concluded not surprisingly that having a job makes an important contribution to happiness, but that genetic makeup is also relevant: Extroverts are happier than introverts. Family life and friends are important, too, as are good health and one's position relative to one's peers.[14]

Buddhists believe that people's dispositions differ and — this is very important — that regardless of their disposition at birth, everyone can improve the way they are. For example, someone who is a pessimist can strengthen his self-confidence through training the mind, which in turn increases his happiness. Buddha said, "Self-confidence is the greatest treasure man can have." He also said, "The master should assign tasks to the workmen in accordance to their abilities."

This is an area where a company can make an important contribution. When people succeed in reaching the goals they or others want them to meet, self-confidence grows. Companies working in this way will increase the self-confidence of their employees and as a consequence their happiness. In this way pessimism is reduced and optimism increased.

WHAT ORGANIZATIONS CAN DO

Many companies have started to realize that they must make it easier for employees to devote more time to their families and other interests. New ways of working have been developed and many more people work part-time. However, it is almost impossible to do that for positions that involve directing people or leadership. Many people accept that if they opt for part-time work they may earn less and have lower prestige within the company, but are happier that way. This kind of career diversity is to be encouraged.

Organizations have the capacity to help create job satisfaction, and beyond that to have an appreciation for the need for happiness among their people. What can an organization do, in terms of policies and values, to spread that happiness? Here is a shortlist of ideas:

❖ Conduct satisfaction surveys of employees to gauge how positive or negative people are feeling about the organization's policies and procedures, and especially about the way management behaves. Take corrective action based on the results to raise morale and job satisfaction (one element of happiness).

❖ Invest in training and personal development programs for employees. This conveys a message of both respect and trust, contributing to an employee's sense of satisfaction.

❖ Make sure that employees understand how they are contributing to the success of the organization at whatever level they work. Also make sure that they feel the company is aware of and appreciates their contribution.

❖ Commit to wealth creation for all employees, including reviewing pay policies and structures, doing away with unnecessary imbalances, and rewarding all contributors to success.

❖ Create corporate responsibility statements for company employees to abide by. These can include environmental policies that address overconsumption or waste of material goods. "Export" such policies to overseas partners and subsidiaries to promote equity and wealth creation in new markets. (There is more on corporate responsibility in Chapter Six.)

❖ Engage in responsible advertising of products and services that does not promote a pure consumption-based economy; appeal to the higher-level needs of the consumer. Avoid creating impressions that are not true and that promote unwholesome consumption.

❖ Consider any downsizing plans carefully. Loss of jobs, and therefore income, can lead to widespread unhappiness. Take all available steps to prevent such an occurrence or at the very least assist employees in finding new jobs. Keep their collective wellbeing in mind.

❖ Lead by example. As a leader, take the opportunity to show satisfaction with life by exhibiting a trained mind and balanced lifestyle.

And, as we shall see in Part III, there are many opportunities to help other businesses and organizations get started and develop by transferring knowledge. In that way an organization can help solve some of the problems of poverty, injustice, and environmental sustainability throughout the world.

We often say in Buddhism that people should free themselves of wants. By "wants" we mean insatiable desires. Buddha said, "You should be satisfied with what you have but never be satisfied with the amount of good you have carried out." We do not see anything beyond happiness because in the Buddhist tradition, genuine happiness can only be achieved by people who act perfectly virtuously, who have no negative thoughts and emotions. We do not mean by happiness a passive feeling of quietude.

Buddhists recognize that acquiring wealth is one of life's fundamental activities. Consumption and acquiring wealth are natural, but if done the wrong way they lead to suffering. Someone who consumes for the sake of consuming without any restraints will not be happy. Buddha recommended that in prosperous periods part of one's gains should be set aside to deal with lean periods. If wealth is earned dishonestly it means stealing from others, or causing other forms of harm. If wealth is not used to benefit other people, it will not provide any happiness for the owner or anybody else. In order for it to lead to happiness, wealth has to be earned honestly and put to good use.

I have listened to and participated in endless discussions on whether profit should be the only purpose for business. For me the answer is simple. Profits are a condition for survival, but their purpose is to make a contribution to the wellbeing of society at large.

CHAPTER SIX

DOING BUSINESS RIGHT

IN BUDDHISM WE believe that the reputation of a company depends on whether it operates with a warm and strong heart. A person who has a warm heart is actively concerned with the wellbeing of others, someone who follows Right Conduct. And good actions are as important for a company as they are for a person; perhaps even more so, since many people are affected by the actions of a company.

As we saw in Chapter Four, humility is one of the character traits of a good leader. Flashy, egocentric chief executives are more likely to prioritize their own interests and pleasures over acting as a good citizen with an interest in the wellbeing of shareholders, employees, and customers. When leaders show tendencies to bad or unwholesome actions, such as dishonesty, they steer their organizations into a position of risk. The consequences of a poor reputation are often hard to overcome.

When I read about corporate scandals, the main causes appear to be craving for power, wealth, or fame by the chief executive. This craving leads to dishonesty and law breaking. If you think back to the basic principles of Buddhism that we discussed earlier, there are warnings about the suffering that comes about from uncontrolled desire or craving. The leaders involved in these scandals lost control over their minds and have become victims of their own negative tendencies. I consider this a great shame, as many of these leaders no doubt have talent and are harming themselves and others without any good reason.

In a sense, the system is to blame as well. Take the example of pay disparity. I find it very disturbing that the heads of companies earn many millions of dollars while some of their employees receive salaries that deny them a decent standard of living. I accept that people with great artistic, physical, or entrepreneurial talent can become wealthy, but this is a very small and unique group. The only way to truly solve this problem is for leaders to exercise self-restraint and, again, to consider the wellbeing of everyone in their decision making.

Some organizations, oil companies for instance, face difficult ethical dilemmas. It is unrealistic to expect these companies to limit their activities to countries with good governance. They will have to cope with weak governments, poor regulation, insecurity, and corruption. They will have to carry out some of the tasks that a government should normally take care of. Given their influence, however, they should make extra effort to make the best of a difficult situation. This would mean, for example, refusing to participate in large-scale corruption.

Within their own organizations, global companies should strive to operate at the very highest level of integrity. They should choose suppliers in their markets that are willing or already operating at a high level of responsibility. This will reward those organizations that have the best interests of society at heart.

DOING WHAT IS RIGHT

Being seen as a company with high ethical standards has enormous value, in tangible and not so measurable ways. Such a company finds it much easier to attract and keep top-class employees. If clients or customers have a positive opinion of a company, they are likely to continue buying from it. Furthermore, loyal customers not only continue to buy but promote the company by word of mouth and other means, thereby contributing to its sustained profitability and growth. A company with an image of high quality and good service can charge a higher price for its products. People are also more willing to try a new product from a company they trust than from an unknown company, or from a company with a questionable reputation. The share price of a company with a good reputation tends to be higher than a one with the same financial performance and a poor reputation. Such a company can borrow funds at a lower rate of interest. Employees' pride in an organization is all the better if it is perceived to be ethical. The list goes on.

A good reputation is the most important immaterial asset that a global company can have, and it has become much more difficult to develop and maintain because of the rising expectations of the public, the critical media, and the oversight of many watchdogs; companies are vulnerable at every turn. Nothing can destroy the value of a company more quickly than the public exposure of grossly dishonest behavior by its top management.

THE CAUSES OF PUBLIC MISTRUST

If you ask the general public their feelings on big business and its leaders, chances are they will respond with some negative or cynical impressions of the "corporate machine." Recent business scandals and underfunding of retirement and pension funds have led to a widespread distrust of business in general.

Leaders should be alert to several practices that are particularly alarming to the public, as outlined below.

Creative or fraudulent accounting

There have been a number of recent examples of companies falsifying accounts, knowingly giving wrong information to the public, or engaging in price fixing, forms of corruption, or insider trading. Such scandals occur all over the world: think of ABB, Ahold, Christie's, Daewoo, Enron, Hoffman-La Roche, Hollinger International, Parmalat, Sotheby's; the list goes on. In almost all instances the CEO is directly involved, which underscores the need for the type of leader we describe in this book. Even though the punishment can be quite severe, involving huge fines and prison sentences, it is unrealistic to expect that these scandals will totally disappear. The pressure for these CEOs to provide increasing profits is paramount. Until the role of the organization is reframed as something greater than maximizing shareholder value, the risk of fraud will remain. It is important to remember, however, that only a small percentage of all companies engage in this kind of practice.

Increasing disparity in compensation

Many people think it is unfair that the compensation of top managers is increasing much more rapidly than that of other employees, especially in comparison with those with the lowest pay. People largely accept that a successful entrepreneur, entertainer, or sports person can make a lot of money, but consider it immoral when the compensation of professional managers keeps rising much faster than that of other employees. For example, the average compensation package of the top CEOs in the US has increased from $480,000 to $8 million in the last 25 years. The average worker's pay is now $27,000, a figure that over the same period has hardly kept up with inflation.[1]

Companies have been unable to convince people that they are acting fairly in this matter. One of the problems is that having a competent and inspiring CEO is fundamental for a company to be successful, yet such people are not easy to find. Those who are able to turn around a declining company, like Carlos Goshn at Nissan or Lou Gerstner at IBM, are "stars" and can command astonishing compensation packages. It is important to remember, though, that these stars are only a very small percentage of the total number of CEOs. If companies and boards are able to exert more control over compensation, it may lead to improved morale and therefore better results in the end.

One interesting development has been at American Express, where chief executive Ken Chenault's pay package now includes an option on 2.75 million shares. However, he will only receive the full grant of shares if AmEx's performance reaches some very high targets – for example, an increase in revenue by at least 10% a year – over the next six years, a long time horizon. This ties compensation closely to performance and is an approach for other companies to consider.[2]

Exploitative practices

There is a danger of exploitative practices in industries such as oil and mining. Ironically, several of the largest oil and gas companies, such as Royal Dutch/Shell and BP, are among the most active in implementing the principles of social responsibility and corporate citizenship, an area we shall consider in more depth later in this chapter. But such companies have made several widely publicized "errors," particularly in the area of environmental violations. BP created headlines with a large oil spill in Alaska, resulting in fines by the authorities. Shell was involved in the now famous Brent Spar debacle, as we shall see in the following section.

The very nature of mineral, gas, and oil exploration and production is exploitative, which makes it difficult to maintain ethical practices. Minerals and oil reserves are found in several poor countries. Often they cannot be sold inside the countries concerned and have to be exported. The potential benefits that the natural resources might contribute to the country may be "stolen" by an economic elite in cooperation with or as part of the government. Instead of being a blessing for a country, such resources often turn out to be a curse.

That said, there are positive steps that companies can take. Many oil companies, when starting a new project, conduct an environmental and social impact study before reaching a decision to proceed. Lately some companies have included in these studies representatives of the communities that will be affected by the project. Large companies are also investing significant R&D effort in the area of renewable energy. It is the task of making the public aware of those efforts that remains difficult.

Marketing of harmful products

In Chapter Two, we talked about the Buddhist principle of Right Livelihood, a component of which is to urge companies not to engage in the production of harmful products. Yet, there are still legal products that are considered harmful to the public's wellbeing and many would argue that if there is a gap in the market, a free-market system will naturally fill it. Nevertheless, the risk to reputation is great for companies in such industries.

Consider the tobacco giant Philip Morris, which after many lawsuits and other PR problems suffered such a setback that it is still trying to dig itself out of the hole. Add to that the fact that smoking has become an unpopular and virtually taboo activity in many countries and Philip Morris finds itself needing to recreate its image yet again, positioning itself as an educational institution on the perils of smoking in the first place. It's an odd spot for a company to be in, promoting a product on the one hand and campaigning against its dangers on the other, but the power of public opinion has made it a necessity.

Human rights and environmental violations

In this age of globalization, many international organizations are being taken to task on their labor practices in developing and poor countries. Watchdog groups are continually alert for both human rights and environmental violations. Companies must be willing to make clear their policies in both areas and apply them to both official partners and unofficial vendors as part of their agreements and contracts. Without these assurances, they run the risk of being associated with practices that ultimately will cost them their reputation.

THE CREDIBLE CORPORATION

Certainly there are many extraordinary leaders who are trying to implement policies that by their very nature will encourage the public to see a company as ethical and credible. The onus is on businesses to win back the favor of society and to change people's expectations of what business can contribute. We are not talking about PR or "spin" here, but about what a company actually *does*.

If the public has a propensity to generalize all big business as malevolent, even companies seeking to do good will fight an uphill battle. Below we describe a couple of ways to help organizations better establish their credibility in accordance with the principles of Right View and Right Conduct.

Promote corporate citizenship

Corporate citizenship, as we saw in Chapter Four, is the idea that a company must act as a responsible member of society, much as an individual citizen should. An important development in this area is the publication of the stock-market performance of "good" companies in rankings such as the Dow Jones Sustainability World Index, Dow Jones STOXX, FTSE4Good Global 100, and the FTSE4Good Europe 50.

Companies have to qualify to be included in these indices by proving that they act in accordance with principles of social responsibility. And these principles are continually evolving to meet developments in corporate responsibility thinking, as the following figures from the FTSE4Good factsheet demonstrate[3]:

❖ *Over 200 companies globally have responded to more stringent environmental criteria to improve their practices, with 85 being deleted for not doing enough to meet the challenge.*

❖ *58 companies have moved to meet the new tougher human rights criteria, with only 20 being deleted.*

❖ *20 companies to date have improved their policies, management*

systems and reporting on supply chain labour standards, with 2
being deleted.

On an international level, the Organization for Economic Cooperation and Development (OECD) has published guidelines offering "recommendations to international business for conduct in such areas as labour, environment, consumer protection and the fight against corruption"[4] and the United Nations has established the Global Compact, described as "the world's largest, global corporate citizenship initiative."[5] According to a survey published in the *World Bank Report 2005*, 20% of companies indicate that the OECD guidelines have influenced their business and that figure is around 30% for the Global Compact. Organizations that are able to demonstrate their adherence to such principles gain a substantial boost to their credibility, as well as benefiting society at large.

Nevertheless, adherence to such guidelines should be reflected in the actual actions of the company rather than merely its PR. A survey by McKinsey reported some interesting statistics[6]:

❖ *More than 90 per cent of CEOs are doing more than they did 5 years ago to incorporate environmental, social and governance issues into strategy and operations.*
❖ *72 per cent of CEOs said that corporate responsibility should be embedded fully into strategy and operations, but only 50 per cent think their firms actually do so.*
❖ *59 per cent of CEOs said corporate responsibility should be embedded into global supply chains, but only 27 per cent think they are doing so.*

Accept that honesty and success can coexist

Many businesspeople claim that business is a fight to the death with their competitors and that in such a situation there is no place for ethics. You have to win or die. They also claim that there is not much room for honesty. Most people do not want to say openly that they act dishonestly, perhaps believing that they are "decent," or at least as much as the next person. They also maintain that any businessperson who disagrees with this view either does not acknowledge the real world of business or is a hypocrite. Of course this kind of behavior and talk gives business a poor image. But the conversation can be changed.

More and more, companies are seeking to operate in an ethical manner and be recognized for their actions. *Ethisphere* magazine recently selected 100 of the "World's Most Ethical Companies" from thousands of candidates. While the inclusion of some of the companies on the list was controversial, the ranking followed an extensive process of screening and measuring. Alex Brigham, the magazine's executive editor, explained:

We looked for absolutes. We examined companies in relational context of their industries. And we looked for influential leadership that moved others to change or follow. Companies were measured in a rigorous eight-step process and then scored against nine distinct ethical leadership criteria… These organizations go beyond making statements about doing business ethically; they translate those words into action.[7]

One organization on the list is Fluor, a Texas-based Fortune 500 company that provides engineering and procurement services, largely to the US government. As the reputation of one of its competitors, Halliburton, has become tarnished with claims of corruption and cronyism, Fluor's is on the rise. Alan

Boeckmann, Fluor Corporation's Chairman and CEO, explains that "ethics and ethical behavior are core values at Fluor and have been since our inception more than a century ago."[8] And the company has the profits to show for it.

Sandy Cutler, CEO of Eaton Corporation, a diversified industrial manufacturer that is also on the *Ethisphere* list, believes that rather than seeing ethics as a compliance issue: "It's about doing business right through internal philosophies and customer commitments. We'll lose business before we will compromise our values." He comments that if a company is committed to doing business ethically, "you can cut the top off and the bottom would keep working."[9]

AIMING FOR VIRTUE AT GE

The world has changed. Businesses today aren't admired... There's a bigger gulf today between haves and have-nots than ever before. It's up to us to use our platform to be good citizens, because not only is it a nice thing to do, it's a business imperative. Good leaders give back. The era in which we live belongs to people who believe in themselves, but are focused on the needs of others.[10]

Jeff Immelt, Chief Executive, GE

General Electric (GE) is one of the world's most prominent companies, with 320,000 employees of whom about half work outside the United States, with a market capitalization of US$375 billion at the end of 2007. Its chief executive until 2000, Jack Welch, was considered one of the most competent managers of our time. Many people doubted that his successor Jeff Immelt would be able to maintain the same high level of performance. To the pleasant surprise of GE watchers, Immelt was highly successful; an even greater surprise was that he told the 200 members of top management that it would take "virtue" to keep the company on top, in addition to having "great people," "growth," and "excellent execution."

Why did Immelt add the goal of attaining virtue? One reason was to improve GE's reputation and lessen reputational risk. No natural disaster can reduce the value of a company as fast as a reputational problem. Recall how Arthur Andersen, an accounting firm with 70,000 employees, virtually shut up shop overnight after its reputation became tarnished in connection with the Enron scandal in the US. As another example, 40% of the market capitalization ($9 billion of the market value) of Marsh McLennan, a large insurance and financial institution, disappeared when it was accused of making profits dishonestly.

The second reason for promoting virtue is that an increasing number of institutional investors are demanding to know if a company is acting responsibly in all aspects of its operations. It makes for a more marketable stock.

The third reason is to motivate GE's employees. Employees prefer working for a company that, as Immelt says, "makes a difference, a company that is doing great things in the world."

Perhaps the most important reason is GE's ambition to be excellent in all it does. Every year, the company organizes a three-week program for executives in their 30s and 40s who are expected to become GE leaders in the future, taking up different themes each time. In 2002 Immelt asked the group to study corporate social responsibility. Its members asked a large number of prominent companies, investors, regulators, and activists about GE's reputation in relation to social responsibility. The result was very negative, GE ranking quite low compared to other large companies.

Known for its incredible speed of execution once a decision has been made, GE instituted a training program to make all employees aware of the importance of virtue. Management started a crash course to improve environmental performance in the company's own activities and acquired a maker of solar-energy equipment, a water-purification company, and a wind-energy business partner. GE performed audits of its suppliers in the developing world to make sure they complied with environmental, health, and labor standards. As a result, it decided not do business in Myanmar (Burma), because the government was a notorious human-rights violator. It started dialogues with socially responsible investment funds and in 2004 was admitted to the Dow Jones Sustainability Index and became one of 300 best-in-class companies.

Immelt knows that complex change requires a focal point in the organization with a person responsible for driving the change. He therefore appointed a vice-president for corporate citizenship, reporting directly to him.

GE is also a strong believer in the merit of diversity among its employees. The company won high-profile awards for promoting women and African-Americans into its executive ranks. People in GE's African-American Forum asked Immelt whether the company could do more in Africa. Although he could not identify a business to be located on that continent, he did decide to invest US$20 million in a healthcare project in Ghana, a country in which GE does almost no business. He said that he could justify such a project without any return on investment in several ways:

❖ *If you look at the long term there is a decent chance that the continent of Africa becomes a market that we want to understand.*

❖ *For young African-Americans, there's an incredible fascination with Africa. They view this as extremely positive.*

❖ *We do this project because GE wants to be known as a good company not just in the US but around the world.*

"Virtue" refers to moral excellence in action. It is the same as what Buddhists refer to as Right Conduct. When the managers at GE were asked to find out what its reputation was in the field of social responsibility, the company showed itself to be serious about finding out the way things really are; that is, the reality or Right View. I am convinced that if many other businesses did the same they would also be disappointed in their results, and more corrective action would be taken.

GE is not just making pious statements but taking action by putting somebody in charge, and implementing educational programs and audits. This shows that its leadership is effectively using the principles of Right View and Right Conduct.

"GULLIVER AND LILLIPUT" AT SHELL

The Brent Spar was an oil storage buoy, 167 meters tall (almost twice as high as Big Ben) and owned by the Shell Oil Company. With its tanks empty it weighed about 14,500 tonnes, roughly the size of a large cross-channel ferry. Shell no longer needed the buoy and, after obtaining approval from the British government, planned to sink it in the North Atlantic. Protests by the environmental organization Greenpeace and media coverage forced it to abandon this plan.

Heinz Rothermund (Managing Director, Shell UK Exploration) commented:

Brent Spar has transformed our outlook. Spar is not as many believe an environmental problem, rather it will go down in history as a symbol of the industry's inability to engage with the outside world. [11]

Rothermund recognized that Shell had failed to consider the effect of its actions on the public at large, and that it would be necessary to do so in the future. He indicated that Shell could have reacted by blaming governments, caving in to violent protests, or accusing Greenpeace of presenting incorrect evidence (for which Greenpeace apologized after the event) – or it could have done some soul searching. It opted for the soul searching. Shell concluded that this situation could be repeated and that its decisions should be made differently. The company found that it needed to be more concerned about the reaction of society at large to its actions. It also had to accept that many people would not trust the statements it made about its environmental performance: It is not a question of "tell me" but "prove it to me."

Cor Herkströter, then Chairman of the Committee of Managing Directors, made the following commitment:

We hope by our future actions to show that the basic interests of business and society are entirely compatible – that there does not have to be a choice between profits and principles.[12]

Shell was among the first companies to put the principles of ethical behavior into a document and to encourage employees to apply them.

Another consequence of the Brent Spar incident was that Shell embraced the principle of "engagement," meaning involving the input of different organizations outside the company in its decision-making process. These external organizations do not have formal authority over the decisions that Shell eventually makes, but they do have an important informal influence because Shell listens carefully to their opinions, explains its own views in return, and engages in a constructive dialogue.

In an article written 10 years after the Brent Spar debacle, Country Chairman of Shell UK James Smith wrote:

We had learned that, while good science and regulatory approval are essential, they are not sufficient. We needed to engage with society – understanding and responding to people's concerns and expectations… We have to consult as early and fully as possible and be willing to listen and change. We must admit mistakes and demonstrate both that we try to put things right and to learn.[13]

THE ROLE OF NGOS

As can be seen from the Brent Spar example, the media and nongovernmental organizations have a great deal of influence on the reputation of business. Without the actions of Greenpeace, the Brent Spar incident would never have hit the headlines. Not only did this NGO exhibit more power than Shell, in this case it also forced the governments of the UK and Germany to abandon their chosen courses of action. This last point was made very clear by Chris Fay, Chief Executive of Shell UK:

Shell UK had been ordered by its parent company, the Royal Dutch Shell group to abandon deep-sea disposal, because other European subsidiaries were finding themselves in an untenable position… The Shell Group has had to react to its failure to persuade ministers in certain European governments to adhere to treaties they are party to.[14]

Most NGOs see their responsibility as looking after the public good, not the good of business. By and large, they concern themselves with large global companies, less so with small to medium-sized businesses. And their actions have a great influence on how the public views the companies they hold under the microscope. Unfortunately for companies, the credibility of NGOs with the public at large is considerably higher than that of global businesses.

Most NGO employees are intellectually bright, good communicators with strong moral convictions. Given these characteristics and the sometimes substantial size and geographical spread of NGOs, it makes them important actors in the global economy. Most large companies are taking a constructive approach to them, although this does not mean that they will do whatever NGOs think is best. It means that they engage NGOs in constructive dialogue and in some cases give contracts to NGOs to undertake studies for them. For example, telecommunications company BT contracted an NGO to study the consequences of outsourcing some of its UK activities to India. When sports apparel marketer Nike found that its inspectors were unable to uncover unacceptable treatment of workers among its suppliers, it engaged an NGO, which found the problem quickly. The employees did not trust the company inspectors but did trust the NGO.

As was true in the Shell case, NGOs and the media reinforce each other. NGOs are skillful in mobilizing media interest and together they have a very strong influence on the reputation of companies, making it essential for businesses to understand how they operate.

The growth and influence of NGOs form an interesting phenomenon. I must admit to having a bias for organizations that are looking after the public good, but I do have a concern that NGOs do not take a holistic view, that they are narrowing in on a particular cause most of the time. It is unreasonable to ask them to understand business better than the leaders themselves. However, if by questioning actions the importance of Right View and Right Conduct is highlighted, this benefits everyone.

In the Shell case, it appears the company lacked humility. Its managers thought, "We know best, we've studied the alternative disposal methods, we've received the approval of the government of the UK. What more could one ask?" This worked against them. The question Shell should have asked was: "How will people react when they find out that we are sinking a large, dirty steel structure in the sea?" If the leaders at Shell had been humble, they would have realized that they did not know the answer and should have sought it out. If Shell had organized a study as Immelt did at GE, to find out public opinion about Shell and its environmental performance, the company might have been warned in time.

As for government leaders, they too lost contact with reality — and again, by "reality" I mean seeing things the way they really are. Neither the governments nor the company had foreseen the strong feelings that a large number of people had about the "holiness" of the sea. Emotional reactions are a part of reality. If strong emotions are involved they should be dealt with constructively. In this case people became angry, and significant effort was required to deal with that anger. From that point of view I am sure that the idea of "engagement" is right. Engagement takes a considered view of the situation and determines whether it requires careful handling. Regardless of where the leadership is coming from, society's wellbeing should be put first.

Ω

The challenge is for business to explain to the public that "good" companies do exist. Organizations should band together in that effort. If leaders lay out their principles and then act authentically, the reputation of businesses will improve, and one of the benefits will be more loyal customers.

When I started this project I was not sure that companies could act in such a way that they could deserve a thoroughly good reputation. Now I am convinced that they can. And I consider this goal very important for individual organizations and for businesses as a whole as one of the most important parts of society.

The task of leaders who want to create positive change for all is among the most challenging and yet rewarding in the world. If the result is companies with a warm and strong heart, much more satisfaction with life and happiness will be the result.

PART III

LEADING IN AN INTERCONNECTED WORLD

Leadership that acknowledges universal responsibility is the
real key to overcoming the world's problems

CHAPTER SEVEN

THE CHALLENGE OF GLOBALIZATION

T HE WORLD IS becoming increasingly interdependent and that is why I firmly believe in the need to develop a sense of universal responsibility. We need to think in global terms, because the effects of one nation's actions are felt far beyond its borders. The acceptance of universally binding standards of human rights is essential in today's shrinking world. Respect for fundamental human rights should not remain an ideal to be achieved but be a requisite foundation for every human society.

Artificial barriers that have divided nations and peoples have fallen in recent times. The success of the popular peoples' movements in dismantling the East–West division, which had polarized the whole world for decades, has been a source of great hope and expectations. Yet there still remains a major gulf at the heart of the human family. If we are serious in our commitment to the fundamental principles of equality – principles which, I believe, lie at the heart of the concept of human rights – today's economic disparities can no longer be ignored. It is not enough merely to state that all human beings must enjoy equal dignity. This must be translated into action. We have a responsibility to find ways to achieve a more equitable distribution of the world's resources.[1]

I am, in principle, in favour of "globalization" and the concept of "global" companies. In the past communities and countries could live in isolation if they wanted to; that is no longer the case. A stock-market crash on one side of the globe can have a direct effect on the other side. Terrorism can be born in one country and destabilize another country far away. Isolation has become impossible. It is my opinion that global companies play an important role in globalization and can be a force for good.

Globalization is seen by many people as a negative development, as a cause of increasing inequality, the benefits of which are gained by large companies and people who are already wealthy. It is seen as leading to a loss of jobs in prosperous, developing, and poor countries alike, and as a cause of legal and illegal immigration, contributing to unemployment and increasing crime rates. The risk is that governments will implement policies that hinder rather than foster globalization.

As I see it, a major cause of the growth in opposition to globalization is resistance to the fact of impermanence, that everything keeps changing. Changes that used to occur over decades now take place in less than a year, and people are not used to such rapid change. Nevertheless, accepting change as a permanent and inescapable aspect of life is very important.

Dealing constructively with globalization, with all its ups and downs, is one of the most important challenges that companies and governments face. It is clear that both have to manage the process much better so that it truly is and is also perceived to be a positive development.

FROM TRADING COMPANIES TO GLOBALLY INTEGRATED ORGANIZATIONS

The oldest global companies were, simply put, *trading companies* that imported and exported goods. A newer type of global company emerged at the end of the nineteenth and beginning of the twentieth century when organizations began to build satellites in other countries, so that they could reduce transportation and import costs and also gain a better understanding of their customers. Another very important motivation was to avoid being forbidden to export through pressure by national companies on the government. Although these *multinational companies* operated in several countries, the home country was by far the most important. Now, an increasing number of companies see themselves as *globally integrated enterprises*, or "citizens of the world." In many cases a company moves successively through these three stages. For example, Toyota started by exporting cars to France; next it built a production factory at Valenciennes, followed by a design center in the South of France, where the Yaris model was created.

The Dalai Lama considers the move to globally integrated enterprises as a positive one.

These three types represent three levels of interdependence when it comes to communication and dependence between individuals. In import and export, contacts are at arm's length. They only involve buyers and sellers. In the satellite type, the satellite company is totally dependent on the parent company in the mother country. The degree of interdependence is much more intense. The communication between the parent company and its satellites includes communicating about production methods, personnel policies, technologies, and relations with the government in a foreign country. The managers and employees from different countries with different cultures have to work effectively together to succeed. The interdependence of the parent company also changes. Its performance becomes dependent on the way it operates not only in the home country but also in the satellites.

The globally integrated enterprise is the first type that I would refer to as being based on a "holistic concept." The starting point is no longer a national parent company with satellites, but a global parent company that aims to realize its purpose by carrying out tasks where they can be executed most effectively regardless of where that might be on the globe. If such a company applies the principles of corporate citizenship or corporate social responsibility, discussed in Part II, it will give equal consideration to stakeholders in all countries where it operates.

It appears to me that as a consequence of interdependence, globally integrated enterprises become more vulnerable and less vulnerable at the same time. If one of their factories is destroyed by fire, there is a good chance that another factory can take over the task. That makes the *entire* company less vulnerable. On the other hand, if the success of a project requires the effective cooperation of organizations all over the world, people must be able to depend on each other. That requires a high level of trust across borders, which I view as a benefit of globalization. If one of the participating units is not performing well, the consequences will be felt by the entire company, increasing vulnerability for all. Maybe this is a positive motivating factor when people realize that their success depends totally on others. When people clearly see how dependent they are on each other, they will feel and act more responsibly.

It is a challenge to replace the work that is done in the home country in harmony with building up activities in other countries. Following Right View means carrying out activities in the locations that lead to the best results for the company as a whole. Decisions should be made from a holistic point of view, considering employees, shareholders, and other stakeholders in all affected countries. This is a hugely complicated process. Impermanence manifests itself in huge changes, like opening and closing factories, setting up additional research facilities in developing countries, and realizing that the best solution next year will not be the same in five years' time. In this context the principle of looking at decisions from multiple perspectives is very important: from the short, medium, and long term, and in relation to exchanging self for others. For instance opening a factory is usually positive; closing a factory is usually negative. Both are unavoidable, a part of impermanence. The task of the leader is to minimize the negative impact of closures. Some irresponsible companies just walk away, whereas responsible organizations make an enormous effort to help people they can no longer employ to find jobs.

For example, a company in Taiwan that had to close a factory but was unable to find work for redundant employees went as far as to start a new activity to provide employment. In Sweden a shipyard closed when it could no longer compete with yards in Korea and Japan. The government and the company together developed a program to stimulate entrepreneurship among the employees to create nonsubsidized secure employment. This involved training people in how to set up and run a small business. Such an attitude avoids a negative impact on the image of the company and reduces harm overall.

STRENGTH IN DIVERSITY

I see as one of the most important challenges in the world today the establishment of harmonious relationships between people of different cultures – races, religious affiliations, tribal identifications, and genders. A significant problem is that some minority groups have dominated society and used their position to gain economic benefits, while other minorities have been discriminated against for centuries. Their unwillingness now to tolerate such discrimination is understandable, but it is sad that it is a cause of violent conflict in many instances. I have witnessed this in India with the caste system. Discrimination must be stopped, but stopping it in the right way is a major challenge.

Buddha considered respect for all to be very important. Buddhists believe that even if a person acts badly, he or she has the potential to become a good person and deserves respect as a human being. The basis for a harmonious relationship is respect, respect for all people regardless of their cultural background. A Tibetan monk who had been tortured by the Chinese told me, "I could cope with the physical pain. My greatest concern was that I would no longer see the torturer as a fellow human being."

Nelson Mandela expressed the right attitude to cultural diversity in this way:

On 27 April 1994 the people of South Africa founded a nation on the pledge that we would undo the legacy of our divided past in order to build a better life for all. It was not a pledge that we made lightly. For generations, millions had been deliberately reduced to poverty... For decades we had fought for a non-racial, non-sexist society, and even before we came into power in the his-

toric elections of 1994, our vision of democracy was defined by the principle, among others, that no person or groups of persons shall be subjected to oppression, domination or discrimination by virtue of race, gender, ethnic origin, colour or creed. Once we won power, we chose to regard the diversity of colours and languages that had once been used to divide us as a source of strength.[2]

Given the importance of dealing with cultural diversity in the right way, I was interested in finding out more about how globally integrated enterprises are coping with this issue. I was pleasantly surprised that some see the cultural diversity of their employees as a significant benefit.

> In 2005 the IBM Corporation, under the leadership of CEO Samuel Palmisano, was the first company to publicly announce its application of the "citizen of the world" concept.[3] It had concluded that innovation was necessary on a global scale and that the satellite model of a parent company and dependent subsidiaries was no longer viable.
>
> As one example of the way this concept works in practice, IBM has taken to heart its value statement that "We are sensitive to the needs of all employees and to the communities in which we operate." It has developed detailed responsibility statements throughout its supply chain, holding its partners to the same high standards set by its own leaders:
>
> *Within our supply chain relationships, we know that our company's sizable purchasing power is a unique resource that we must manage responsibly, and we do. IBM spends nearly $2 billion a year with diverse suppliers, for example, greater than any other technology company. Yet more than managing our spend, we have a responsibility to hold ourselves – and our suppliers – to high standards of*

behavior. This means complying with all applicable laws and regula-
tions. But it goes beyond that. It entails a strong commitment to work
with suppliers to encourage sound practices and develop sound
global markets.

We have always maintained an open channel of communica-
tions with suppliers to set expectations. Today, in an increasingly
interconnected world market, the expectations for all players across
the entire supply chain go up. Therefore, we are both reaffirming our
existing policies and instituting some new practices, which are spelled
out in [our] Supplier Conduct Principles. These principles establish for
our suppliers the minimum standards we expect from them as a con-
dition of doing business with IBM. IBM will have the right to take
action with suppliers that fail to comply with these principles, includ-
ing terminating our relationship with them.

Our goal is to work with our suppliers to foster full compliance
as they, in turn, apply these to their extended sources of supply
engaged in the production of goods and services for IBM. We will
consider these principles and adherence to them in our selection
process and will seek ongoing compliance by actively monitoring
performance.[4]

IBM was the first US company to put country nationals rather
than Americans at the head of its European companies. The
rationale for cultural diversity was expressed by Palmisano as
follows:

Diversity in IBM is a business imperative. Our customers are diverse;
therefore we must understand their diversity by knowing who they
are, how they think and what they want. IBM cannot claim that it is
dedicated to every client's success unless it understands their clients.
And those clients cannot be understood unless IBM has employees
from the same diversity groups.

Diversity is also the cornerstone for innovation. According to IBM studies, 50% of GDP growth in the US in the second half of the twentieth century was based on innovation. Innovation used to take place in Western countries and be exported to other parts of the world. That has changed. Innovation has become global in two ways. First, when a new product comes onto the market it is available globally. Good examples are mobile phones and PCs. Second, innovation depends on insight and invention. Insight requires an understanding of the global marketplace and invention requires as many constructive innovative inputs as possible. A company with a diverse workforce can generate far more perspectives and insights than can a monocultural group of white men. The experience of IBM is that to innovate rapidly one has to have a process that is collaborative, multidisciplinary, and global. Working effectively across borders and cultures requires trust between employees and between the company and the market. Trust can only be built on the principle of respect for others.

Adopting diversity as a goal has many consequences. An example of IBM's tolerance of different cultural practices is that as the number of Muslim employees grows, the company is converting offices in the US and Canada into prayer rooms, and restrooms have been redesigned to include cleansing stations for Muslim employees' prayer preparation.

GE is another leading global company that sees the world as its home. CEO Jeff Immelt said: "We are committed to performance and to being a good global citizen... Every day we take actions that align our performance ever closer with the standard of what it means to be a good and trusted citizen." GE has come to the same conclusion as IBM, as the following statement shows:

GE must become more like their customers. That means more Chinese, more Indians, more Blacks, more women especially in the top ranks.

Make no mistake: Creating an effective and harmonious relationship between people from different backgrounds is a huge challenge. The main problem is lack of trust. When operating in a known environment people have a good idea of whom they can trust. They are not so confident about this when dealing with people from a different culture.

We have to face the reality that many groups of people have been told for centuries that they are superior to members of other groups, or that some other people are dangerous to associate with. It takes time to eradicate those prejudices. Many people maintain it will take several generations, but I do not agree. Global companies show that positive results can be achieved quite quickly.

COMPETITION IS A MEANS TO AN END

One result of globalization is increasing competition. Competition generates a very powerful force to produce what people want at reasonable prices. But it is a means, it is not an end. The end is to generate benefits for all. So why is it so difficult to arrive at fair competition and an equitable distribution of those benefits?

Competition generates wealth. If leaders of businesses are only interested in enriching themselves as fast as possible with little or no regard for any harmful consequences for others, then competition is being used in the wrong way.

If we disregard such obvious bad actions as selling dangerous products or making dishonest claims about a product, the three most harmful competitive practices are eliminating competition by establishing a monopoly position, price fixing, and corruption. These practices are illegal in most countries but are still widespread. Governments must play a role in stopping such activities and maintaining real competition.

Governments themselves are also involved in distorting competition, especially at the global level, by subsidizing their national companies and establishing trade barriers to protect these companies from competition. Most subsidies in prosperous countries are now applied in the agricultural sector, but governments face the problem that if they radically reduce these protections in a short space of time, this can lead to a high level of unemployment.

Another factor that leads to unfair competition is lobbying by business of government officials. Businesses have a right and a duty to inform government about matters that are relevant to a policy the government wishes to implement, but often businesses or their associations are not considering the consequences of a policy for the public at large but only from their own point of view. This is clearly an example of adopting a self-centered perspective, of wrong view.

One more point on competition: Many people only see competition and do not realize that there is a very large degree of cooperation as well. The ability of a company to compete depends on effective cooperation between all of its employees. Furthermore, the company may have to cooperate with a large number of suppliers. In addition, even many competitors cooperate in areas such as setting safety and performance standards. Unfair and dishonest competition does take place, but it is possible to compete while respecting ethical standards.

When we face reality, it is obvious that we cannot imagine a modern society without competition as a fact of life. I do not claim that in this book we outline all the answers to making competition work effectively for everyone. I do believe, however, that many of the suggestions we have already made about following Right View and Right Conduct can create a more positive form of competition. This is also the case when considering the world's environmental problems.

MEETING THE ENVIRONMENTAL CHALLENGE

The challenge for global companies is to become pioneers in making the world a better place to be, particularly when a combination of rapid growth in population and increases in the standard of living are threatening the viability of our planet. When we look for organizations with capabilities and the ability to get things done, global companies are on the top of the list, in particular globally integrated enterprises, which are in an ideal position to help developing countries catch up with developed countries. Global companies also have the competence and resources to solve environmental problems, given the right governmental framework.

Wind turbines in India[5]

Tulsi Tanti, an Indian engineer, managed and owned a small textile company. His profits were reduced by regular failures in the electricity supply. He bought two wind turbines to generate power and solve the problem. In 2000 he read about global warming. As he said: "I suddenly had a very clear vision. If Indians start consuming power like Americans the world will run out of resources. Either you stop India developing, or you find some alternate solution." That is an example of Right View.

As an example of Right Conduct, Tanti sold his textile business and entered the wind turbine field as a business. By 2007 he had become the fourth largest wind turbine maker in the world, with revenues of $850 million. He commented: "Yes, green business is good business. But it's not just about making a profit. It's about being responsible." He started by selling wind turbines, but soon realized that the buyers were not really interested in buying wind turbines: They wanted a reliable energy supply. He changed his business model to sell energy instead and organized financing, installation, and maintenance himself. Without this innovation he would never have succeeded as he did.

Tanti pulled off an incredible feat by buying a German wind turbine producer, RE Power, for US$1.7 billion. The French company Areva, one of the most powerful power companies in the world, controlled by the French government and managed by one of the best managers in France and with revenues of US$13.7 billion, already owned 30% of RE Power. Tanti said: "I can take a company with a 4% profit margin and turn it into a company with a 20% margin. Areva can't. So I knew from the beginning: whatever they offered, I could pay more." That illustrates a saying of Buddha: "The greatest treasure man can have is self-confidence."

Now Tanti runs a truly global company: the power stations are designed in the Netherlands, the turbines are manufactured in Germany, and the heavy steelwork and installation are handled in India. The wellbeing of all those involved has improved. The reason Tanti is exceptionally successful in India is the poor functioning of the country's electricity supply. Getting a reliable energy supply justifies paying a higher price than would be the case if India had a reliable power delivery system. There is no need for government subsidies.

Carbon credits in an outcast community[6]

Another example is also from India and shows how globalization helped to move subsistence farmers from abject poverty to a decent standard of living and contributed to reducing the problem of global warming. It is an example of how innovative thinking and right motivation can achieve excellent results. Those involved were the World Bank, a paper mill, a small Indian NGO, and a leader with the right motivation and enthusiastic effort.

The scheme happens in one of the poorest areas in India where half the people belong to the lowest caste, or more precisely are "Untouchables" or outcasts, the poorest of the poor, with an illiteracy rate of 90%. These people live in chronic poverty and are barely able to survive. But poor as they are, they do not want to relocate. Surprisingly, 60% of their land is uncultivated. Under the scheme the farmers plant trees in the uncultivated land, sell the trees to the paper mill, keep the branches to use as firewood, and are paid for the carbon credits they produce. The scheme, which took four years to get off the ground, will eventually cover 3,500 hectares (around 8,500 acres) and provide an escape from abject poverty for 3,000 subsistence farmers.

The plan would have never succeeded without the leadership of Masabathula Satyanarayana, a professional with a forestry background. He says: "Carbon finance is my passion." He realized that reducing the impact of global warming and using carbon credits can lead to an increase of forest coverage.

A tree type had to be found that was suitable for growing. Fortunately, the paper mill believed in sustainability and had selected a type of eucalyptus that was right for both the environment and papermaking. The paper mill guaranteed to buy the trees after four years, a guarantee that was necessary for the farmers to borrow money. Another obstacle was the farmers' lack of knowledge and self-confidence, which was solved by training. The project leader said:

These farmers have always been poor, so were their ancestors. If you experiment and it goes wrong there's no cushion, it's a disaster. We have to spend a long time building their confidence, demonstrating how it will work.

Finally, to make the project really attractive the World Bank had to be convinced to award carbon credits that could be sold. That was also a long and difficult process and came close to failure because the World Bank feared that the management capabilities in the project were too weak. Again, Satyanarayana's perseverance and self-confidence saved the project.

Examples such as these are encouraging, but much more has to be done to avoid environmental catastrophe. We are together responsible for what happens and will happen in the world. Each of us has some influence on what will happen. If we think we are powerless we have reached a stage of despair. Despair has never solved anything. The problems in the world are not imposed by some outside force but are our responsibility.

Global companies, when they feel and accept this universal responsibility, can make a contribution far greater than the products they sell and the direct benefits they deliver to their employees, clients, shareholders, and other stakeholders. Organizations and governments together can play an important role in helping to solve environmental problems and in making people more concerned for the wellbeing of others, not only in their own country but throughout the world.

CHAPTER EIGHT

ENTREPRENEURSHIP AND POVERTY

P OVERTY IS A huge problem in developing and poor countries. But poverty is a problem of the mind, not of lack of resources or lack of intelligence of the people. If all people, organizations, and governments applied the principles of Right View and Right Conduct, rapid progress would result.

Four conditions are necessary to make such rapid progress. First, the government of a country must be motivated to improve the wellbeing of all citizens and not only of an economic elite or of the members of government. Second, the economic system has to be developed along the principles of a responsible free-market economy (described in Chapter Nine). Third, regulations must stimulate entrepreneurship. Finally, voluntary family planning has to be introduced more successfully to reduce the rate of population growth.

As a consequence, the population will shift from agriculture to manufacturing and service, the cities will grow, and the number of people living in rural areas and working in agriculture will decline. Extreme poverty is concentrated in rural areas. It is impossible to solve the poverty problem without people moving from the countryside to cities. This can, however, only be achieved if people can find decent jobs in the cities. This transition requires the acceptance of impermanence by all citizens. If people are not willing to move and change jobs, it is impossible to solve the poverty problem. The same applies to family size.

Jobs can only be successfully created through entrepreneurship. Buddha recognized entrepreneurship as a valuable activity. He encouraged entrepreneurs to be successful by being reliable and having an eye for what would sell. He also suggested they should save money for a rainy day and share some of the results with their employees.

According to Buddhism, the first task of every householder is to take care of themselves. Only after doing that can a person start to take care of other people. Making economic progress depends on "adding value." As we saw in the example about reforestation in the previous chapter, when subsistence farmers produced trees in addition to food their prosperity increased. If poor farmers continue to work as they do now, they will remain poor for ever. Ingenuity can add value, but in most cases the budding entrepreneur needs capital. If in the reforestation case the farmer had not been able to borrow money based on the contract with the paper mill, the project would have failed.

A woman who stitches dresses by hand in a poor country will be very poor. If she buys a sewing machine she can produce more and will earn more. And if she is a more talented entrepreneur and can sell more dresses than she can produce and employs other women to work for her, her prosperity will increase further. It is a very simple process. When moving up the scale, knowledge and education become increasingly important.

Entrepreneurship is an excellent way to be able to take care of oneself and others when it comes to providing a decent standard of living. Poor people consume very little because they earn very little. If they earn more they will consume more. Entrepreneurship is by far the most effective method to enable people to earn more and become participating members of an economy. Governments can stimulate entrepreneurship by poor people through many measures, for example by assigning property rights to those who live in slums, or making it easy to register and start a business in a legal way. This is the Right View. The wrong view is that people in developing countries are lazy, unwilling to work, and only think of tomorrow.

No matter what part of the world we come from, we are all human beings. We all see happiness and try to avoid suffering. We have the same basic human needs and concerns. All human beings want freedom and the right to determine their destiny as individuals and as peoples, and in order to do so we need the opportunity to rise above abject poverty. It is human nature to want such things and it is within our power to provide them.

SHIFTING PERSPECTIVE

After becoming independent in 1947, India pursued a policy of self-sufficiency and import substitution, meaning that instead of importing products it developed its own industries to build the domestic economy. This policy was executed by heavy government involvement, by determining which products to produce and where to manufacture them within the country. Very little business activity could take place without the initiative or approval of a government department in Delhi, otherwise known as the "license raj" system. This restrictive policy and some other factors led to a financial crisis in 1991, at which time the government asked Manmohan Singh, a Sikh with a PhD in economics from Oxford, to become Minister of Finance. Dr. Singh accepted and very quickly diagnosed the problem. He told the Prime Minister:

We are on the verge of an economic collapse. It is possible that we will collapse, but there is a chance that if we take bold measures we may turn around, and turn it into an opportunity. We must convert this crisis into an opportunity to build a new India.[1]

Dr. Singh then told the parliament:

Victor Hugo said, "No power on earth can stop an idea whose time has come." We can follow the traditional way, tighten our belts, tighten and tighten, but if we do that it will lead to more misery and more unemployment. There is an alternative path. The idea whose time has come is that India should emerge as a major global and economic power. This alternative path is economic stabilization and a "credible structural adjustment program."

What was this "credible structural adjustment program"? The program consisted of abandoning the policy of import substitution and opening India to imports, encouraging entrepreneurship along the way. In Dr. Singh's words:

We got the government off the backs of the people of India, particularly off the backs of India's entrepreneurs. We introduced competition, both internal competition and external competition. We made risk-taking much more attractive and much more profitable. So we tried to create an environment conducive to the growth of business. We removed a large number of controls and regulations, which in the past had stifled the spirit of innovation and the spirit of entrepreneurship, and restructured the scope of competition, both internal and external. As the result, in the 90s productivity increase in the Indian industry has been much faster than ever before.

Although the details at the time were slim, Dr. Singh said afterwards in an interview:

My dream was that as we were in a crisis, that we should undertake basic structural changes. Out of that would emerge a new India, an India where there will be no poverty, the freedom from poverty, ignorance, and disease. You get that with India becoming a major global player in the world economy. That was the vision that inspired our economic reforms.

Dr. Singh had presented a vital policy change: relying on entrepreneurs to create jobs and not on government departments; and recognizing that in order to achieve that, entrepreneurs need freedom. He also identified the critical elements, that none of this would succeed without provisions for making it easy to start a business in a legal way, securing property rights, and ensuring judicial independence and impartial courts. We will return to these points later in this chapter.

The economic reforms that Dr. Singh referred to were heavily influenced by what he had observed happening in South Korea. South Korea had started from a similar position to India in 1950. Along with some other East Asian countries, it had succeeded in one generation in transforming the character of its economy, eradicating chronic poverty in the process. South Korea put more emphasis on basic education and healthcare, priorities that have not taken hold in India's transformation.

In his exile in India, the Dalai Lama witnessed the country's development at first hand.

Dr. Singh changed the economic policies that had been established by Nehru, the first Prime Minister after India became free. I met Nehru several times and was always impressed by his kindness, in word and action, for us Tibetans, as exiles in his country. He also gave me the impression of being a highly intelligent person with the interest of all Indians at heart, and so I interpret his role in the economic crisis as one of having good motivation.

Dr. Singh provides an excellent example of what we could call "the ability to shift perspective." This refers to the capability of viewing a problem from different angles. In so doing a person can change a threat into an opportunity, as Dr. Singh did. When I speak of adopting a wider perspective, this includes looking at a situation from different points of view — the personal level, the community level, the country level, the economic perspective, the wellbeing perspective, the government perspective, the business perspective, and from a short- and long-term vantage point.

When you have a crisis that is global by nature, such as environmental degradation or problems in the economic structure, a coordinated and concerted effort among many people, with a sense of responsibility and commitment, is an absolute necessity. Of course, change must start from within the individual, but when you are seeking global solutions you need to be able to approach these problems from the standpoint of the individual as well as from the level of society at large. For leaders, finding solutions requires fostering a flexible and supple mind. When facing a problem like Dr. Singh's, the leader needs a very high level of knowledge and competence to identify the right perspective — and then to act on it.

HELPING ENTREPRENEURSHIP TO FLOURISH

Two of the necessary conditions for stimulating entrepreneurship are that governments have the right motivation and that the right regulations be established and implemented. These two aspects are linked. For example, a government with the wrong motivation will not establish the right regulations; and indeed, in such countries you may find government officials living in luxury in the midst of widespread poverty. The right motivation means that the government sees its role as looking after the wellbeing of all the citizens of the country, especially the poor.

Facilitating business start-ups

It sounds strange, but the fact is that it is much more difficult for an entrepreneur to start a business in a poor country than in a prosperous one. In many poor countries it is almost impossible for an entrepreneur to set up a business in a legal way: It takes too long, is too complicated, and costs far more than they can afford. The only way is to operate in the black market, and indeed in many poor countries the size of the black market is greater than the official market. The facts are well known, but governments in poor countries have great difficulty in changing the law, often because of economic and professional elites who make their money from giving approvals for business start-ups – lawyers, professional institutions, and a large number of government departments that all want to be paid, officially and often unofficially.

A government must have the courage, self-confidence, and lack of fear to face down vested interest groups like an economic elite and to act in the interests of society at large. The preoccupation of professionals and government employees with the resulting loss of income can be understood, but their situation will be much better once the economy starts to flourish through successful entrepreneurship. Lawyers and accountants are well paid in prosperous countries, after all.

Securing property rights

Secure property rights and the belief that the courts will uphold those rights are very important for increasing investment and productivity in a given market. Companies and individuals act differently when they own a property and feel safe in the knowledge that it cannot be arbitrarily taken away. Consider the case of China, which has moved from a communist system where households did not own any land and where all the production belonged to the state to a system where farmers can obtain a 30-year lease and can sell a portion of their product in the "free" market. The effect of these reforms has been a significant increase in output, about half of which was ascribed to the changes in land rights.

Anybody visiting a large city in a poor country will notice the slums on its outskirts. The people living there are very poor and are likely to have moved from rural areas to the cities to find work. They start living in the most primitive conditions on open land, where it is not clear if anybody has property rights or not.

Electricity and water companies are often not willing to provide these basic services to those without property rights. In addition, such people are at the mercy of low-level community employees who demand bribes so the poor can stay where they are. If the government or community decides to give rights to the minuscule plot to the family living there, the status of those people changes dramatically for the better. And when they are owners it is beneficial for them to improve their very rudimentary dwellings.

This change can be more powerful than providing micro-credit (on which there is more to follow) – the value of these small plots is far in excess of the size of a micro-credit loan and offers many other benefits.[2] But implementing such a change demands courage from the government, since many people both inside and outside government profit from these poor people's lack of basic security.

The problem of property rights is not limited to private entitlements but also to the property rights of business, or intellectual property. Many companies do not believe that the courts will uphold their property rights; in fact, a 2005 study by the World Bank concluded that businesspeople in Indonesia, Tanzania, India, Pakistan, Brazil, Poland, Russia, and Peru had a very high lack of confidence in obtaining a fair interpretation of the law, in most cases higher than 50%.[3] The World Bank found this lack of confidence to be related to the time required to enforce a contract. In Pakistan and Brazil the process of enforcing property rights could take years and considerable financial resources.[4]

I visited a government office dealing with property rights in Jaipur in India. The files were stacked three meters high and three meters deep without any space between the stacks. With such a system it is impossible to find out what the rights for a particular property are. The only people who can find out are those who can pay for an official to start digging. Fortunately, the Indian government has solved this problem. These deeds are being computerized and anyone can ask to see them for a very low standard fee.

This reminds me of a supposedly true story about the practice of law in an isolated community in the Himalayas. When a lawsuit was brought to the court to decide, the court followed a very simple procedure: The person who paid the highest bribe was always judged to be right. These bribes were used to organize parties in which all citizens participated, but the judges and other members of the elite had the best seats at the table, the finest food and drink, and the most lavish presents.

Giving title to land, houses, and ideas has a very positive impact on reducing poverty, increasing investment, and creating jobs – and yet progress is slow. Governments must be very determined to carry out such entitlement programs and to oversee judicial systems to uphold them.

Having a fair, functioning banking system

Some countries only have only state-owned banks. These banks are rarely efficient or fair.

In 1991 when I first visited Dharamsala, where the Dalai Lama has his residence, there was only one branch of the state bank of India. It was open for four hours a day, five days a week, and if at 4 p.m. there was still a queue outside waiting to be served, the staff just closed the doors. You were, even as a foreigner, treated as trouble. This has changed completely, however. There are now several private banks and you can change currency 18 hours a day, 7 days a week – better than in many prosperous countries.

Big banks are not as yet equipped to deal with small loans, but for entrepreneurs needing only modest amounts of money, micro-credit has proven an excellent solution. The concept of micro-lending or micro-credit is fairly new and was conceived with a relatively narrow definition: the extension of small loans to entrepreneurs too poor to qualify for traditional bank loans.[5]

There are many differences between micro-credit and regular lending practices, but some of the more salient distinctions are:

❖ It recognizes and promotes credit as a human right.
❖ It is not based on any collateral or contracts, but rather on trust between the parties involved.
❖ Efforts are made to keep the interest rates at low levels rather than pursuing the goal of high returns for lenders and investors (the typical credit model).[6]

In short, micro-credit is based on the idea that the poor have skills that are underused. It is not for lack of skills that people end up as poor; it is for lack of opportunity and accessibility. It is also based on the premise that poor people are trustworthy and diligent about paying back their loans, perhaps more so than others, often out of a sense of gratitude and obligation. Breaking down the stereotype of unreliability is one of the most critical steps in the fight against poverty.

Over the past three decades, Muhammad Yunus and the Grameen Bank of Bangladesh have developed the use of micro-credit as a critical tool in ameliorating the plight of the poor worldwide. The concept has been so successful that Professor Yunus and the Bank were jointly awarded the Nobel Peace Prize in 2006 with the recognition that "Lasting peace cannot be achieved unless large population groups find ways in which to break out of poverty. Micro-credit is one such means."

Some people make the mistake of thinking that micro-credit alone can solve the problem of poverty, however. Micro-credit makes an important and essential contribution, but for entrepreneurship to function an efficient and fair ordinary banking system is required.

Another organization that takes the concept of micro-credit but expands on it is BRAC, established by Fazle Hasan Abed in 1972 to help Bangladesh overcome the devastation caused by the war with India. BRAC's objectives are "poverty alleviation and empowerment of the poor." While the organization believes that micro-credit is an important tool for breaking the poverty cycle, it also trains its members in income generation and helps them link to markets for their goods. Its holistic approach begins with women as the primary caregivers, and combines micro-credit with health, education, and other social development programs.

BRAC's Economic Development program organizes almost 5 million poor people, mostly women, and has operations in around a dozen countries, including Africa, the Middle East, Afghanistan, and Sri Lanka. In addition to the provision of credit and savings accounts, there are human rights and legal education courses, legal aid clinics, and household visits by volunteer health workers. The Health, Nutrition and Population program provides basic health services to more than 97 million people, including control of infectious diseases such as tuberculosis, acute respiratory infections, and diarrhoea, and advice on preventive health measures. The aim of poverty reduction through education is addressed by the Non Formal Primary Education program, which has almost 50,000 schools containing a high proportion of those traditionally excluded from formal schooling, particularly girls. The Adolescent Development program gives training in vocational skills, health awareness including reproductive health, and leadership.[7]

Reducing the rate of population growth
In 2002 I joined 136 other spiritual leaders from 31 countries – Roman Catholic, Protestant, Muslim, and Hindu – in sending a letter to President Bush to encourage him to continue to provide funding for the voluntary family planning provided by the United Nations' Population Fund (UNFPA). I wrote in that letter, "Family planning is crucial, especially in the developing world." Another Nobel Peace Prize winner, South African Archbishop Desmond Tutu, wrote, "Planned parenthood is an obligation of those who are Christians. Our church thinks we should use scientific methods that assist in planning families."[8]

This is not only an economic issue. It is a question of freedom and the right of women to be able to decide how many children they wish to have and when. No man has a right to force a woman to have a child that is not welcome.

In Buddhism we consider every life to be precious. However, the population explosion is ultimately a very serious matter. So family planning is crucial, especially in the developing world.[9]

When you read in the newspapers about the ravages of illness, natural disasters, internal wars, HIV/AIDS, and lack of food in poor countries, you might expect that the population there is stagnating or even declining. The opposite is in fact the case: the poorer the country, the faster the population growth.

I will try to illustrate this with a few examples.[10] The US has the highest rate of population growth among prosperous countries. In 2006 it had a population of 300 million. That is the same as Pakistan, the Congo, and Ethiopia added together. Assuming that the birth rate (the average number of children per woman) remains the same in each country, by 2050 the US population will have grown to 420 million. The other three countries together will have increased to 690 million; that is, 270 million more than the US.

What about other statistics relating to the same three developing countries? Infant mortality – that is, the number of children who die under the age of 1 per 1,000 live births – is 80, so 8 out of every 100 children die within their first year. Life expectancy is 46 years. And 80% of the population in these countries live on less than US$2 per day.

All these countries have inadequate infrastructures – poor roads; power that is only available intermittently; lack of safe drinking water and no sewage system; insufficient schools, hospitals, and medical doctors. They all need to make huge investments in these areas, as well as investing in training and paying for qualified teachers and doctors to provide their people with a decent standard of living and to bring down infant mortality rates and increase life expectancy substantially. As the population grows so does the size of the investment needed. Even wealthy countries with low rates of population growth have difficulties in financing their infrastructure and healthcare requirements.

Let us look at another example. In 2006 there were 60 million people in the UK and 75 million in Ethiopia. In 2050 the UK will have 70 million inhabitants and Ethiopia 145 million; that is, more than England and France combined. Think what would happen if the population of the UK doubled by 2050.

China has been very successful in reducing its birth rate per woman, which was down to 1.6 in 2006. However, to do this it employed what some regard as extreme measures, limiting couples to one child. A second pregnancy may result in a fine, "encouragement" to have an abortion, or even forced sterilization. In contrast, a very poor state in India reduced its birth rate as fast as China's using education rather than coercion. Kerala is a large district with approximately 35 million inhabitants. The birth rate was reduced from 4.4 in the 1950s to 1.8 in 91. How did it achieve this? Four actions were taken: the encouragement of good basic healthcare, facilitating many women to work, encouraging men to respect women, and open and informed public discussion. The important variables are education, job opportunity, and nondiscrimination against women. The conclusion is that birth rates can be reduced without coercion, but doing so requires major changes in attitudes and values. The Right View is that each couple should aim to have no more than two children for the world population to be at a sustainable level.

The Dalai Lama is very concerned about poverty and about the risk that the world might run out of natural resources. He considers that life is holy, but is convinced that in the situation the world faces today and in poor countries in particular, it is absolutely necessary to reduce the birth rate.

Fortunately, governments in practically all very poor countries consider their birth rates too high. However, they have difficulties in doing anything about it. The Dalai Lama considers it very important that a reduction is achieved only by using peaceful means; that is, by convincing men and women to reduce family size. Kerala's example is one that many countries may find it beneficial to follow. Reducing the birth rate does not require a large investment – it is a question of education and a change in attitude.

COLLABORATION BETWEEN BUSINESS AND GOVERNMENT

Solving the problems of poverty requires a combination of action by central and local government, contributions from prosperous countries, and help from responsible global companies. South Korea has demonstrated that a country can be successful in eliminating poverty in one generation if the government is competent and in charge of the transformation process. Only a national government can establish an environment in which entrepreneurship will flourish, raising the impoverished out of unacceptable conditions.

Global companies with the right motivation can find ways to act that are beneficial for themselves, the countries in which they operate, and also for the poor. I am in favor of wealthy people and companies contributing to charities. But it is clear to me that much faster change can be achieved when a company finds ways in which it can create employment and stimulate entrepreneurship among the poor, helping them to expand their own businesses and make a profit. The problems of poverty are so severe that it is impossible to solve them in a few years. Therefore, it is all important to start as many new initiatives as possible that enable the poor to earn a decent living.

Shakti in India

Unilever, a global supplier of nutritional and personal care products, reaches customers around the globe every day. Beyond this basic business objective, the company views two other goals as important: the creation of wealth for the company and for society in its markets, and minimizing the negative environmental impact of its operations.[11] Unilever has recognized that stimulating entrepreneurship among the poor is essential to creating wealth and reducing poverty. In particular, the company has recognized the benefits to both the company and society of creating new entrepreneurs and jobs in India, Indonesia, and other countries.

To expand its markets, the challenge for Unilever's business in India was how to reach millions of potential consumers in small, remote villages where there is no retail distribution network, no advertising coverage, and poor roads and transport. The solution was Project Shakti (meaning strength in Hindu), launched in 2000 in conjunction with nongovernmental organizations, micro-lending banks, and local governments. In many of the villages women have formed self-help groups. Unilever made a presentation of its Shakti scheme to these self-help groups to find women who would like to become entrepreneurs.

The easiest way to understand how Shakti works is by looking at an example. Rojamma, from a very poor family, was married at 17 to a man with whom she had two daughters but who then left her to fend for herself. She earned a few rupees working in her mother's field, but found it almost impossible to survive. Unilever made a presentation to her self-help group offering members the opportunity to sell and deliver the company's products in her village. Rojamma accepted the job.

Unilever provided training in sales skills and book-keeping to enable Rojamma to become a fully fledged micro-entrepreneur. The company helped her borrow 10,000 rupees (US$200) at favorable conditions to invest in a stock of goods at the start-up of her business. Rojamma visits her clients carrying products to sell. The target is to have about 500 customers. She sells about 10,000 rupees' worth of stock per month and makes a profit of about 800 rupees (US$16; average agricultural wage rates for women in India are 30–40 rupees a day). Rojamma said, "When my husband left me I had nothing except my daughters. Today everyone knows me. I am someone. It also has enabled me to send my daughters to school, a chance I did not have."

In 2006 the system was operating effectively in 50,000 villages and involving over 30,000 women. Unilever's goal is to establish 100,000 Shakti entrepreneurs by 2010, reaching 600 million people in 500,000 villages.[12]

Innovating for the common good

One of the most prominent NGOs, Oxfam, carried out research with Unilever into the company's impact in Indonesia. This was an important study, one of the most extensive evaluations jointly conducted between a company and an NGO.

Indonesia is a country that has been making substantial progress. It is very populous, with a population of 225 million that will rise to 285 million in 2050, close to that of the USA in 2006, and a birth rate of 2.4. Around 50% of the population live on less than US$2 per day, which is similar to China but much better than India.

Oxfam and Unilever decided to carry out a joint project to evaluate the impact of Unilever's activities in Indonesia and whether these helped or hindered in the fight against poverty.[13] Oxfam approached this with a positive but skeptical attitude about the activities of global companies. Both recognized each other as serious organizations and there was mutual respect.

The study took more than a year and examined the impact of the whole value chain, from relationships with small-scale producers to interactions with low-income consumers, as well as employment policies and practices, and the wider impact on the community.[14] At the end both organizations had a much better understanding of the limitations and opportunities that determine what companies can and cannot be expected to do to contribute to poverty reduction.

The study found: "Of the total value created, around two-thirds is distributed to participants other than Unilever Indonesia, such as producers, suppliers, distributors, retailers and the Indonesian government." However, it concluded:

Participation in value chains such as Unilever Indonesia's does not automatically guarantee improvements in the lives of people living in poverty. For supply and distribution chains to benefit poor people even more, there need to be other social institutions and resources in place such as credit and saving schemes, marketing associations, and insurance schemes.

Oxfam stated:

Many companies still see their purpose as profit maximisation, but we have learned from Unilever that in many cases business decisions rarely amount to a strictly profit-based calculation. The notion that the business of business is business is outdated. There are huge opportunities to innovate for the common good.

This is an example of facing reality for both Oxfam and Unilever, which began from different perspectives. They wanted to find out the truth and they overcame their fear on both sides that it would have a negative effect on their reputations.

The interdependencies in Unilever's relationships in India and Indonesia are very obvious. This represents a typical example of Right View. It is one-sided to look only at the profit Unilever is making; the other participants are also making a profit. You could say that profits make the system sustainable. As soon as any link in the chain is suffering a loss, the vitality of the total system is endangered.

I am also interested in the willingness to share knowledge. Sharing means that a person can decide to give or not to give knowledge to others. Unilever is giving away a large amount of knowledge: about how to become an entrepreneur, make high-quality products, and develop more efficient production methods. This transfer of know-how is beneficial for the recipients but also for Unilever. When it comes to profits, however, I do not think that it is a question of Unilever sharing its income with others. All participants in the system make a profit in their own organizations and share in the additional value they have created together with Unilever.

REGULATION AND FREEDOM

Freedom in connection with regulation is an interesting concept. What is freedom for one person may be a limitation for another. For example, the very strict regulations that a pharmaceutical company must follow before it is allowed to sell a new drug impose many limitations on a business. It takes five to ten years between the discovery of a new drug and the date that the product can be sold to the public at large. During these five to ten years the drug must be tested on an ever-increasing number of people. From the consumer's point of view this is very good, because the person who has to take the medicine is free from worry that it might be dangerous. I think that regulations always impose limitations on some actors that represent freedom for others. That is probably the reason it is so difficult to develop regulations that please everybody.

As Buddhists we rarely consider limits to freedom. We believe that when people have the right motivation they will not abuse their freedom. When we speak about freedom we are thinking primarily of freeing ourselves from bad habits, bad thoughts, and bad motivations. People are only free when they are no longer suffering from negative thoughts and emotions. I recognize that a country needs laws to set limits to freedom. I think, however, that it should not be forgotten that many of these laws set limits that would not be crossed by people acting responsibly. Acting responsibly requires more than not breaking the law. I have been pleased to note that several companies in their business principles state that the company will respect not only the letter but also the spirit of the law.

Most people want maximum freedom. It is obvious that freedom without responsibility is not acceptable; it is even dangerous. Total freedom would mean that whoever is the strongest decides, whether their view is right or wrong. Some political leaders, even some intellectuals, have argued that it is a fundamental mistake to protect the weak as it will lead to a degeneration of the human species. Some of these ideas were popular in the regime of Hitler, who believed that the most powerful nation should rule and decide what is right and wrong.

The Buddhist view is that all people have the same rights to justice and a decent standard of living independent of their capabilities and strengths, physical and intellectual, and that actions should be based on Right View and Right Conduct. The view also recognizes that there should be regulations that are enforced. It is clear that you need much fewer regulations when people act according to Right View and Right Conduct. Buddhists accept that in reality there are a large number of people who will not act according to Right View and Right

169

Conduct, and that makes it necessary to have more restrictive regulations than otherwise would have been required. Self-regulation is always superior, but is not sufficient.

Many of the world's problems are ultimately rooted in inequality and injustice, whether economic, political, or social. Ultimately, this is a question of the wellbeing of all of us. Whether it is the suffering due to poverty in one part of the world, or the denial of freedom and basic human rights in another part, we should never perceive these events in total isolation. Eventually their repercussions will be felt everywhere.

The world is getting smaller and everything depends on everything else. Others' interests are actually our own interests also. If others are happy, we will be happy. If others suffer, we ultimately will suffer.[15]

It is important for organizations – whether they be in business, the nonprofit world, or even governmental – to take a leadership role in addressing the huge economic imbalances. I believe the time has now come to address all these global issues from the perspective of the oneness of humanity, and from a profound understanding of the deeply interconnected nature of today's world.[16]

CHAPTER NINE

THE RESPONSIBLE FREE-MARKET ECONOMY

T HE BASIC HUMAN desire for freedom and happiness cannot be subdued. The thousands of people who marched in the cities of Eastern Europe a few decades ago, the unwavering determination of the people in my homeland of Tibet, and the recent demonstrations in Burma are all powerful reminders of this truth. As discussed in Chapter Eight, freedom is the very source of creativity and human development. It is not enough, as communist systems once assumed, to provide people with food, shelter, and clothing. If we have these things but lack the precious air of liberty to sustain our deeper nature, we remain only half human.[1]

I believe that a form of cultural genocide has taken place in Tibet, where the Tibetan identity has been under constant attack. The distinctive cultural heritage with its characteristic language, customs and traditions is fading away. In reality, there is no religious freedom in Tibet. Nor is there any real autonomy, even though these basic freedoms are guaranteed by the Chinese constitution. For nearly six decades, Tibetans have had to live in a state of constant fear, intimidation and suspicion under Chinese repression. Nevertheless, they have been able to keep alive their basic aspiration for freedom. I believe the demonstrations and protests taking place in Tibet are a spontaneous outburst of public resentment built up by years of repression. But I say to both the Tibetans and China, don't commit violence. Our only weapon, our only strength, is justice, truth. If the majority of Tibetans resorted to violence, I would have no option but to resign as spokesperson of the Tibetan people.

China is emerging as a powerful country due to her great economic progress. This is to be welcomed, but economic progress alone will not suffice. There must be improvements in observance of the rule of law, transparency and right to information, as well as freedom of speech.[2]

A democratic system based on freedom is, in my view, the system that can contribute the most to our collective happiness with the lowest level of risk of a serious abuse of power. Democracy creates checks and balances within the government, so that if a leader is found to have bad motivation, or is incompetent, the system can counter the problem. It makes the government aware that its task is to serve the people and not the other way around, and to act responsibly in the process.

Buddha attached great significance to freedom and emphasized the importance of free choice and responsibility. Buddha also repeatedly stressed the importance of discipline, with the idea that greater discipline brings less suffering and more happiness. A core value of people is that they want to be happy. Freedom from coercion is an important part of happiness. For example, if people and the press are denied the right of free speech and expression, the public at large may not be aware that their views are being manipulated by the government or that a business is acting highly irresponsibly before a great deal of damage has occurred. A democracy has the added advantage of being able to hold public debates about alternative courses of action. In this way people are better informed and new solutions can be found. I am talking about functioning democracies, not one-party democracies, or "one-leader-for-ever" democracies, or democracies where the country is in a state of chaos. I also recognize that changing from a nondemocratic system to a properly functioning democracy is a major challenge.

☾

In *The Leader's Way*, we have been talking about how individual leaders can develop new skills and train their minds for more disciplined decision making. We have considered the role of such a leader, how he or she can shape the values and the agenda of an organization. We have also seen how leading companies are making strides in the areas of corporate responsibility, environmental sustainability, and the fight against poverty. All of this exists under the scope of economic and political systems.

In the many discussions I had with the Dalai Lama about the economic and political systems in which visionary leaders and organizations could thrive, he expressed the view that the most successful system should be based on freedom, but also on compassion and concern for the wellbeing of all those within its scope. Such a system, as the Dalai Lama came to realize, has the potential to exist under the umbrella of the free market.

SOCIALISM AND THE FREE MARKET

For much of my life, I was attracted to the socialist or communist system because I understood its objective to be providing a decent standard of living and justice for all. I was drawn to it for its equality; extreme differences in standards of living between people are not to be tolerated. The objective included abolishing poverty and furthering the brotherhood between people within and between countries. Over time, I found out that the countries that practiced the communist system did not reach this objective; they did not even try to. On the contrary, development stagnated and freedom of speech was eliminated. Although I still believe that the initial objective was right, I have come to see the flaws in such a system.

My understanding of the communist system was deepened through the meetings I had with China's communist Chairman, Mao Tse-Tung. In person, Mao impressed me in many ways. When he explained the communist system to me I did not realize at the time that it was a command-and-control system based on central planning of economic activity. He explained it as a system where the capitalists would no longer exploit the workers, which I fully supported. It was not obvious to me that the abolition of private ownership would lead to ownership by the state, with a party elite in charge who would then institute their own restrictive command-and-control system and rule as an elite, like the aristocracies in the past. Of course, we now know this led to many human rights abuses.

Mao invited me to attend one of the meetings with his cabinet. What I especially remember was that he asked the cabinet members for suggestions on how they could improve the performance of the government. Nobody said a word. Mao then pulled out a letter that he had received that described many serious problems the people were facing, leaving me with the impression that he had a sincere interest in the wellbeing of the Chinese people. He came across as a great personality and, for some time, I admired him. What finally changed my mind was that he told me that religion is like poison. He knew that I was a Buddhist, so his comments made clear to me that the friendship he had shown was not genuine.

It is through this process of listening and observing that I have come to put my faith in the free-market system. Although it has great potential for abuses as well, the fact that it allows for freedom and diversity of thought and religion has convinced me that it is the one we should be working from. Of course, I still believe we should strive for an adequate standard of living for all rather than the "survival of the fittest" position that the free market often follows. In this regard, there is something to borrow from the socialist system.

Almost all modern governments have chosen variants of the free-market system; the pure command-and-control economies have all but gone by the wayside. Nevertheless, the issue is not as straightforward as merely choosing a system, as in the case of China.

In the past few decades, China has put its economic goals above its political ones. Its leaders abandoned the communist policies of central planning and control, and reduced state ownership of the means of production. The country identified four areas for modernization: agriculture, industry, the military, and science and technology.[3] In agriculture, rural communities were discontinued and peasants were allowed to lease land and sell their harvest in markets. Special economic zones, such as Shenzhen and Xiamen, were created where foreign investment was encouraged and new factories were established. The military was modernized by reducing the number of soldiers and improving military technology with advanced weapons systems. To boost science and technology, thousands of students were sent abroad, particularly to the United States, to study science and engineering.

Although China has continued to implement free-market policies with great economic success, it has come under increased scrutiny in recent years. Human rights issues continue to be a problem. The country's regulatory and monetary policies are not yet at the same level as other free-market economies. In other words, China demonstrates a bridging of a communist party-based government with a free-market economy. Although the general standard of living has increased, widespread poverty still exists in rural areas and some basic freedoms continue to be suppressed.

LESSONS FROM ADAM SMITH

In 1776, Adam Smith published *An Inquiry into the Nature and Causes of the Wealth of Nations*. Written for governments to "instruct" them in the policies they should implement, *The Wealth of Nations* advocated that society had a moral obligation to see to it that everyone, especially the workers, had a decent standard of living. Smith's conclusion was that this could only be achieved through a free-market system; by "free," he meant that people should be free to buy and sell goods and services in a system established by government.[4] This conclusion was based on two insights: first, that competition would lead to the most effective creation of wealth; and second, that effective competition depended on government regulation. These insights still hold true today.

In Smith's day, however, the government was not seeing to it that there was effective competition. Governments protected industries from competition by imposing tariffs on imports, as well as other barriers such as import quotas. Such restrictions persist today. Adam Smith had observed that businesses would try to short-circuit competition by convincing the government that it was in the national interest to protect them from competition. This had two negative effects: first, the purchasing power, especially of low-income wage earners, was reduced; and second, companies would not be interested in innovation if they could make satisfactory profits without the extra effort of improving their performance or innovating.

Smith also noted that companies in a particular sector often formed associations that acted as pressure groups on the government to seek advantages that would have to be paid for by the public at large. They often also colluded to raise prices all at the same time, or to reduce output below demand so that they could raise prices. It was the task of government to withstand these pressures from business and to stop collusion that artificially raised prices. This pressure on government to distort competition was not limited to companies, but was also exerted by professional organizations and craftsmen who were members of guilds. Smith was not against such associations *per se*, but warned governments that they were not interested in the wellbeing of the public but rather of themselves. He said, "Whenever people or businesses can promote their self-interest at the costs of the public at large they will."

Smith recognized this self-interest as the "invisible hand":

By preferring the support of domestic to that of foreign industry, [every individual] intends only his own security; and by directing that industry in such a manner as its produce may be of the greatest value, he intends only his own gain, and he is in this, as in many other cases, led by an invisible hand to promote an end which was no part of his intention… It is not from the benevolence of the butcher, the brewer or the baker that we expect our dinner, but from their regard to their own interest.[5]

The Dalai Lama recognizes the danger behind this self-interest.

Adam Smith refers to the development of moral sense by imagining oneself in the position of others. That is what we refer to as "exchanging self for others." Unfortunately, Adam Smith did not stress sufficiently the need of people to train in exchanging self for others. Even though he had a keen interest in and insight into moral issues, Smith believed that competition and regulation of competition could lead to prosperity for all. What is missing is to insist that Right Conduct is also necessary. It is not possible by regulation and competition alone to arrive at a decent standard of living for all.

Adam Smith and other economists have concerned themselves with the *generation* of wealth, but do not provide any guidance on the *distribution* of wealth. Karl Marx, on the other hand, looked at this the other way around. He was only interested in the distribution of wealth, not in how to generate it. In my view, both the proper creation of wealth and the right distribution of it are very important. In order to reach such goals one requires the right policies and the application of Right View and Right Conduct.

> In many respects, Adam Smith was ahead of his time. According to him government had many tasks, among them the development of physical infrastructure, the establishment of property rights, and an effective system of justice; topics that we have addressed in Chapter Eight. Property rights he deemed as very important because they make it attractive for people to invest, save, and improve their standard of living.
>
> Another of Smith's concerns, much like the Dalai Lama, was the idea that people would start to believe that ever-increasing wealth would make them happy. He wrote that even though there was the potential for that misunderstanding, the pursuit of wealth at least helped to solve the problem of

poverty. This optimism carried over to other things. Smith believed that it is part of human nature to be pleased when others are happy, even though one gains no benefit from it. He also wrote that moral people do not seek approval, but self-approval that they have lived up to proper moral standards, even when their actions go unrecognized. He lived that way himself: When he died, he left his substantial savings to charitable causes.

WITH FREEDOM COMES RESPONSIBILITY

Much like Adam Smith, Friedrich von Hayek, a well-known twentieth-century economist and proponent of free-market capitalism, recognized that establishing and protecting freedom and liberty in a free-market system is a major challenge:

Freedom and responsibility are inseparable. Many people fear freedom. It is doubtless because the opportunity to build one's own life means an unceasing task, a discipline that man must impose upon himself if he is to achieve his aims. We assign responsibility to a man not in order to say that he might have acted differently, but in order to make him act differently in the future. If I have caused harm to somebody by negligence or forgetfulness, this does not exempt me from responsibility. It should impress upon me more strongly than before the necessity of keeping such consequences in mind. A free society probably demands more than any other that people be guided in their action by a sense of responsibility which extends beyond the duties exacted by the law.[6]

The effect of the free-market system is, as we know, a high level of average income but still unacceptable levels of poverty.

Because of this, Hayek considered it justifiable to take care of the poor. He wrote:

there can be no doubt that some minimum of food, shelter and clothing, sufficient to preserve health, and the capacity to work as well as education, can be assured to everybody without endangering freedom in a society that has reached a general level of wealth as ours.[7]

The Dalai Lama recognizes this shortcoming of most free-market economies and supports a compassionate approach in what he calls a *responsible* free-market economy.

Even though Adam Smith was concerned with the moral dimensions of the economic system, many of his successors ignored that aspect. I consider an economic system without a moral dimension to be dangerous. That is why I want to add the dimension of "responsibility" to "free market." I agree with the concept of freedom advocated by Smith and Hayek, but feel it does not take us far enough.

Responsible behavior is necessary because of the limitations of what can be achieved by laws and regulations. It is impossible for governments to make people behave decently by law. The system will only work well when the leaders of businesses and government have the right motivation and act accordingly. With every action people should ask themselves: Am I acting responsibly? This may sound rather mundane to many people; but anybody can point to a lot of irresponsible behavior around them from others while not recognizing their own irresponsible behavior. And even if they do, they refer to other people acting the same way. Yet when people act responsibly they will be much happier, they will have peace of mind. They will feel that they have done the best they can and will be satisfied.

ACHIEVING FREEDOM AND PROSPERITY FOR ALL

The goal of assuring freedom and prosperity for everyone is a lofty one. Over and over in this book, we have encouraged leaders in business and government to take the initiative in addressing poverty, promoting environmental sustainability, protecting human rights and access to justice, making diversity a strength. It is the Dalai Lama's contention that if all of these matters are actively being pursued, it will translate to greater peace and more widespread happiness for the global population. The Dalai Lama considers the possibilities and the promise in each of these areas, one by one.

The reduction of poverty

When traveling around the world I have been both surprised and dismayed by the very high prosperity in some parts and the abject poverty in others. The number of rich people in the world is growing; yet at the same time the poor remain poor and in some cases are becoming even poorer. This I consider to be completely immoral and unjust.

We need to address the issue of the gap between the rich and the poor, both on a global and national level. These inequalities, with some portions of the human community having abundance and others on the same planet going hungry or even dying of starvation, are not only morally wrong, but practically also a source of unrest.[8]

A sustainable economy

The concept of interdependence is at the heart of environmental sustainability, for it is a fundamental law of nature. The myriad forms of life are governed by interdependence. All phenomena, from the planet we inhabit to the oceans, clouds, forests, and flowers that surround us, arise in dependence on subtle patterns of energy, water, and air. Without their proper interaction, they dissolve and decay.

We need to appreciate this fact of nature far more than we have in the past. Our ignorance of it is directly responsible for many of the problems we face. We have to limit as much as is feasible our consumption of natural resources and move as fast as possible to sustainable development. Allowing unchecked population growth, in developed and undeveloped nations alike, will only put a further draw on our precious resources. And the fight over those resources is a serious threat to sustained peace. We must respect the delicate matrix of life and allow it to replenish itself.[9]

The protection of human rights

All human beings, whatever their cultural or historical background, suffer when they are intimidated, imprisoned, or tortured. It is not enough that the United Nations has defined human rights: They must also be implemented. I think the UN formulation is quite good, however rights depend on responsible action. This is why I put so much emphasis on the word "responsible" in the responsible free-market economy.

Some Asian governments that are now participating in the free-market economy have contended that the standards of human rights used by the West cannot be applied to Asia and other developing countries because of differences in culture and in social and economic development. I do not share this view and I am convinced that the majority of Asian people do not support such an opinion, for it is the inherent nature of all human beings to yearn for freedom, equality, and dignity, and they have an equal right to achieve that. I do not see any contradiction between the need for economic development and the need to respect human rights, as long as these are linked to the obligation of responsible action.

Tradition can never justify violations of human rights. Thus discriminating against people from a different race, against women, and against weaker sections of society may be traditional in some regions, but if they are inconsistent with universally recognized human rights, these forms of behavior must change. The universal principles of equality of all human beings must take precedence.[10]

The strength in diversity

The rich diversity of cultures and religions should help to strengthen the vitality of communities and not be a source of conflict, as is the case in many parts of the world. Underlying this diversity are fundamental principles that bind us all as members of the same human family. I am convinced that all people, regardless of race and religion and gender, have the same innate potential capabilities. I consider diversity to be a very powerful, positive thing.[11]

We as Tibetans have a unique culture that is appreciated by our people and contributes to the store of ideas of other people. One of our unique cultural features is the knowledge we have developed based on the teachings of Buddha. These teachings did not originate in Tibet but in India. That shows the value of access to new ideas from other countries. The sincere appreciation of different ideas is very positive: It enriches the mind. Mahatma Gandhi made a delightful statement on this point:

I do not want my house to be walled in on all sides and my windows to be stuffed. I want the cultures of all lands to be blown about my house as freely as possible. But I refuse to be blown off my feet by any.[12]

A call for universal responsibility

My ideas about universal responsibility have evolved from my studies as a Buddhist monk. Concern for the wellbeing of others compels us to reach out to all living beings. Usually our interest in the wellbeing of others is limited to our family and friends or those who are helpful to us. That is not enough. We should be concerned for the wellbeing of everyone. We can take strong action to defend ourselves against aggressive enemies, for example, but we should never forget that they are also human beings.[13]

Interdependence between countries has increased dramatically through economic integration, easy communication, and low-cost transportation. It has become very old-fashioned to think only in terms of my nation or my country, let alone my village. Governments have the responsibility not only to ensure the future happiness of their own people, but also to cooperate effectively with other countries. I do not believe that we will achieve a borderless world any time soon. However, I have been encouraged by the development of the European Union and how countries have learned to share some aspects of their national sovereignty. I hope that similar developments will occur in other regions. The United Nations is providing some important guidance, and useful action, at a global level. Nevertheless, its capabilities to solve the world's problems are still quite limited. I am in favor of an increase in those capabilities, but of looking toward other solutions as well.

Freedom is precious. Freedom that leads to happiness depends on responsible actions by people as individuals and as members of organizations. Leadership that acknowledges universal responsibility is the real key to overcoming the world's problems.

EPILOGUE

I F YOU REMEMBER only two concepts after reading this book – Right View and Right Conduct – and keep these two principles vivid in your mind, your decision making will improve, as will your satisfaction with life. With Right View you will examine your intentions and make sure that you consider the consequences of your actions on yourself, your organization, and others, and will do your utmost to avoid harm and increase the wellbeing of others. You will also be able to reduce the negative thoughts and emotions that lead to wrong decisions and unhappiness for yourself and others.

When you become a leader your power to influence and ability to get things done grow very substantially. With that boost in power comes an increase in your responsibility for making the right decisions. Making the right decisions in an interconnected world is becoming more challenging all the time. When you are able to keep a calm, collected, and concentrated mind even under intense pressure, you will be better able to reach the right conclusions and consider the consequences from many perspectives – short term and long term, for employees, customers, shareholders, and society at large.

Globalization is a positive development as long as the companies involved act responsibly and their leaders develop a holistic view of their role in society. And organizations are also dependent on governments acting in a responsible manner. Businesses should work constructively with governments to reach the goal of a responsible free-market economy and reject an economic system without moral values.

This book project began with a discussion about integrating capitalism and Buddhism. By the end of the project it had become very clear to me that investments are necessary to create prosperity. Investments require capital. Satisfying the need for capital is therefore very important. The problem with the word "capitalism" was that it made me think of capitalists who exploit workers, thereby becoming very rich while the workers remain poor. This problem has not disappeared altogether, particularly in poor countries.

Capital is a means not an end. The end is freedom and prosperity for all. This can best be reached by a free-market system in which all participants act responsibly. In my way of thinking, integrating capitalism and Buddhism happens when Right View and Right Conduct become an integral part of the economic system. I see the word "responsible" in this context as standing for Right View and Right Conduct, and therefore hope that the words "responsible free-market economy" will come to replace the words "capitalist system."

Inequality in personal wealth is as old as civilized society. With the scientific knowledge, technology, and understanding of the mechanisms of wealth generation now available, achieving a decent standard of living for all has become definitely within reach. My hope is that the ideas presented in this book will inspire many leaders and organizations to work with patience and enthusiastic effort toward reaching that goal.

NOTES

Chapter One

1 The image of the net of Indra is used under a Creative Commons license from from http://commons.wikimedia.org/wiki/Image:Indrasnet.jpg.
2 Robert H. Rosen (2008) *Just Enough Anxiety: The Hidden Driver of Business Success*, Portfolio, p. 15.
3 The company is SHV Holdings NV, the largest privately owned company in the Netherlands, involved in energy, transport, consumer goods, and the provision of private equity.

Chapter Two

1 Sherron Watkins (2006) "Ken Lay still isn't listening," *Time*, June 5.
2 His Holiness the Dalai Lama (2005) *The Universe in a Single Atom: The Convergence of Science and Spirituality*, Morgan Road Books, p. 177.

Chapter Three

1 His Holiness the Dalai Lama (1995) *Awakening the Mind and Lightening the Heart*, HarperCollins, p. 56.
2 His Holiness the Dalai Lama and Daniel Coleman (2003) *Destructive Emotions and How to Overcome Them*, Bloomsbury.
3 Amanda Ripley (2008) *The Unthinkable: Who Survives When Disaster Strikes – and Why*, Random House.
4 Howard Cutler (2001) "The Mindful Monk – Dalai Lama Interview," *Psychology Today*, May.
5 His Holiness the Dalai Lama (2000) *Transforming the Mind*, Thorsons, p. 8.
6 Thubten Yeshe (1995) *The Tantric Path of Purification*, Wisdom Publications, p. 38.
7 Piet Hut (2003) "Life Is a Laboratory," in Allan Wallace (ed.),

Buddhism and Science: Breaking New Ground, Columbia University Press.

8 His Holiness the Dalai Lama (1991) *Cultivating a Daily Meditation*, Indraprastha Press, p. 110.

9 His Holiness the Dalai Lama, Lecture at Kalmuck Mongolian Buddhist Center, New Jersey, www.Circle-of-Light.com/Mantras.

Chapter Four

1 Chester I. Barnard (1939) *Dilemmas of Leadership in the Democratic Process*, Princeton University.

2 Jim Collins (2001) *Good to Great: Why Some Companies Make the Leap ... and Others Don't*, HarperBusiness.

3 Jack Welch & Suzy Welch (2008) "State your business. Too many mission statements are loaded with fatheaded jargon. Play it straight," The Welch Way, *BusinessWeek*, 3 January.

4 The Right Conduct examples come from Vodafone.

5 Chester I. Barnard (1939) *Dilemmas of Leadership in the Democratic Process*, Princeton University.

6 Lama Thubten Zopa Rinpoche is spiritual director of the Foundation for the Preservation of the Mahayana Tradition.

Chapter Five

1 Ven. P. A. Payutto, *Buddhist Economics: A Middle Way for the Market Place*, www.buddhistinformation.com/buddhist_economics.htm.

2 Samyutta Nikaya, I.89ff.

3 Anguttara Nikaya, I.12.

4 Digha Nikaya, 26, the Cakkavattisihanada Sutta and the Kutadanta Sutta. See also Walpola Rahula (2000, revd edn) *What the Buddha Taught*, Atlantic Books.

5 Peter Senge, Foreword to Arie de Geus (1999) *The Living Company: Growth, Learning and Longevity in Business*, Nicholas Brealey Publishing.

6 Arie de Geus (1999) *The Living Company: Growth, Learning and Longevity in Business*, Nicholas Brealey Publishing, pp. 17–18.

7 Universal Declaration of Human Rights, www.un.org/Overview/rights.html.

8 Abraham H. Maslow (1987, 3rd edn) *Motivation and Personality*, HarperCollins.
9 Dhammapadatthakatha, III.262.
10 Fred Hirsch (1976) *The Social Limits to Growth*, Routledge & Kegan Paul.
11 Richard Layard (2005) *Happiness: Lessons from a New Science*, Penguin; Andrew Oswald (2003) "How much do external factors affect wellbeing? A way to use 'happiness economics' to decide," *The Psychologist*, 16: 140–41; E. Diener & R. Biswas-Diener (2008) *Rethinking Happiness: The Science of Psychological Wealth*, Blackwell; Martin Seligman (2003) *Authentic Happiness*, Nicholas Brealey.
12 Bruno Frey & Alois Stutzer (2002) *Happiness and Economics*, Princeton University Press.
13 Mark Honigsbaum (2004) "On the happy trail," *The Observer*, 4 April.
14 Frey & Stutzer, *op. cit.*

Chapter Six

1 Bruce Murphy (2004) "In a generation, gap separating compensation of chiefs, others widens," www.jsonline.com, 9 October.
2 AmEx: Geoff Colvin, "AmEx Gets CEO Pay Right," *Fortune*, 21 January 2008.
3 *FTSE4Good Index Series Factsheet*, 2007, FTSE Group.
4 OECD (2007) *Annual Report on the OECD Guidelines for Multinational Enterprises 2007*, Organisation for Economic Cooperation and Development, www.oecd.org.
5 *What Is the UN Global Compact?* www.unglobalcompact.org/AboutTheGC/index.html.
6 McKinsey & Company (2007) *Shaping the New Rules of Competition*, July.
7 *2007 World's Most Ethical Companies*, http://ethisphere.com/2007-worlds-most-ethical-companies.
8 Fluor Corporation press release, 21 May 2007.
9 *2007 World's Most Ethical Companies*, http://ethisphere.com/2007-worlds-most-ethical-companies.
10 Marc Gunther (2004) "Money and morals at GE," *Fortune*, 15 November.

11 Tony Rice & Paula Owen (1999) *Decommissioning the Brent Spar*, Routledge.
12 *Profits and Principles – Does There Have to Be a Choice?* Royal Dutch/Shell, 1999.
13 James Smith (2005) "Putting what we learned from Brent Spar into practice," *Greenpeace Business*, April.
14 Rice & Owen, *op. cit.*

Chapter Seven

1 Adapted from a speech by His Holiness the Dalai Lama on "Humanity and Globalization" at UNESCO, 8 December 1998.
2 UNDP (2004) *Human Development Report*, United Nations Development Programme.
3 Samuel Palmisano (2005) "Multinationals have been superseded," Financial Times, 11 June.
4 IBM's Global Procurement Policy Statement, www.ibm.com.
5 "Tulsi Tanti: Windpower saved his first factory. Now he wants to harness it to help save the world," *Time*, 29 October 2007; Rebecca Bream & Fiona Harvey, "Suzlon plans to double wind turbine capacity," *Financial Times*, 29 October 2007; "Indian firm wins wind power fight," BBC News, newsvote.bbc.co.uk.
6 Malcolm Doney (2007) *Cutting Carbon*, Department for International Development, Issue 39.

Chapter Eight

1 PBS interview with Dr. Manmohan Singh, 2 June 2001.
2 The originator of this idea was Hernando de Soto, founder and director of Peru's Institute for Liberty and Democracy. Hernando de Soto (1989) *The Other Path: Invisible Revolution in the Third World*, Basic Books; (2001) *The Mystery of Capital*, Basic Books.
3 *World Development Report 2005*. World Bank, p. 246.
4 *Doing Business in 2004*. World Bank, country tables.
5 "What is microcredit?" Muhammad Yunus, September 2007, www.grameen-info.org/bank/whatismicrocredit.htm.
6 *Ibid*.
7 Information on BRAC is drawn from www.brac.net/history.htm.
8 "International Committee of Religious Leaders for Voluntary

Family Planning calls on President Bush to release $34 million for UNFPA," *Progressive Newswire*, 30 April 2002.

9 Speech by His Holiness the Dalai Lama on 28 September 1996, www.dalailama.com.

10 Figures and projections from the Population Reference Bureau.

11 Unilever's corporate purpose statement, www.unilever.com.

12 "Helping Women, Creating Entrepreneurs," www.unilever.com.

13 *Financial Times*, 7 December 2005.

14 Information on this case study is drawn from "Indonesia: Exploring the links between wealth creation and poverty reduction," www.unilever.com and Jason Clay (2005) "Exploring the links between international business and poverty reduction: A case study of Unilever in Indonesia," Oxfam GB/Norib Oxfam Netherlands/Unilever, www.oxfam.org.uk.

15 Comments on Burma by His Holiness the Dalai Lama on a visit to Thailand, 18 February 1993.

16 Excerpted from His Holiness the Dalai Lama's acceptance speech at the Congressional Gold Medal Award Ceremony, 18 October 2007, www.dalailama.com/news.171.htm.

Chapter Nine

1 Adapted from a speech given by His Holiness the Dalai Lama on 21 October 2007, www.dalailama.com/news.174.htm.

2 His Holiness the Dalai Lama, Press Release, 18 March 2008, www.dalailama.com/news.218.htm; Statement of His Holiness the Dalai Lama on the 49th Tibetan National Uprising Day, www.dalailama.com/news.215.htm.

3 *China and the Four Modernizations*, The Library of Congress Country Studies, www.country-studies.com.

4 Adam Smith (1776) *An Inquiry into the Nature and Causes of the Wealth of Nations*, Edinburgh.

5 *Ibid.*, Book 4, Chapter 2.

6 Friedrich F. Hayek (1960) *The Constitution of Liberty*, University of Chicago Press, p. 74.

7 Friedrich F. Hayek (1944) *The Road to Serfdom*, University of Chicago Press, p. 124.

8 Adapted from a speech given by His Holiness the Dalai Lama, www.dalailama.com/page.45.htm.

9 Adapted from a speech given by His Holiness the Dalai Lama,

www.dalailama.com/page.86.html.

10 Adapted from a speech given by His Holiness the Dalai Lama, www.cosmicharmony.com/Tibet/DalaiLama/DalaiLama.htm.

11 *Ibid*.

12 Mohandas K. Gandhi (1980) *All Men Are Brothers: Autobiographical Reflections, ed. Krishna Kripalani*, Continuum International, p. 142.

13 Adapted from a speech given by His Holiness the Dalai Lama in India, www.spiritsound.com/bhiksu.html.

INDEX

Abed, Fazle Hasan 160
accepting reality 23, 25–6
accounting, creative or
    fraudulent 114
acting the right way 14
actions
    bad 29, 44–5
    effect on self and others 22
    ethical 31–4
    good 29, 44–5, 111
    quality of 15
    taking the right ones 13,
    29–46
    unwholesome 32
    wholesome 32
AIG-Thailand 92
Alavi 105
American Express 115
Andersen, Arthur 122
Arrow, Kenneth 15
Asavabhokin, Anant 59

bad actions 29, 44–5
banking system 158–60
Barnard, Chester 71
Boeckmann, Alan 121
BP 116
BRAC 160
breathing technique 56–7, 58
Brent Spar 116, 124–8
BT 127
Buddha
    and self-oriented drives 2
    teachings of 29
    view of happiness 16
    view of poverty 99
    view of suffering 16

view of wealth 95–6
Buddhism
    application to business 5, 16,
    17, 41
    concept of consumption 2
    concept of happiness 2
    concept of self 105
    concept of wealth 2
    concept of work 2
    contribution to global
    economy 41
    emphasis of 13
    fundamental concepts of 5, 8,
    13
    holistic approach to solving
    problems 2
    lack of fatalism of 24
    rational and logical attitude
    of 2
    stress on human values 2
    synthesis with capitalism 7,
    186
    synthesis with concepts of
    Western thinkers 8
    view of death 95
    view of entrepreneurship
    149–50
    view of freedom 171–2
    view of happiness 110
    view of profit 110
    view of wealth 110
Buddhist monks, life of 1, 13
Buddhist philosophy 3, 13, 14
Buddhist principles, application
    of 4, 29, 50–51
Buddhist values, application on
    global scale 9

Bunag, Dhaldol 92
Burma 171
    human rights in 123
business and happiness 102–10
business start-ups, facilitating
    155–6
business
    collaboration with
    government 164–8
    similarity to Buddhism 16

calm, clear and concentrated
    mind 9, 14, 15, 19, 47, 71, 80,
    185
calming the mind 62, 64
capitalism
    synthesis with Buddhism 7,
    186
    ways of improving 4
career diversity 108–9
causality, principle of 19
cause and effect, law of 19, 20
causes and effects, network of
    23
change
    coping with 71
    incremental 18
    inevitability of 9, 14, 22–4,
    27, 134
    positive ways to deal with 24
character of leader 76–9
Chenault, Ken 115
China 89–90, 156, 162, 171–2, 174–6
codes of conduct 73
codes of ethics 73
Collins, Jim 72
communism 173–6
company, as example of interde-
    pendent organization 22
compensation
    disparities in 112, 114–15
    executive 88, 109
competition 176
    fair 142

role of 142–4
    unfair 143
competitiveness 24
concentration 36, 38, 55–6, 59
conditioning 48
conduct, codes of 73
conscience, whether business
    has 100–101
consequences, considering from
    many perspectives 20
consumerism 106
consumption
    Buddhist concept of 2
    wholesome and unwhole-
    some 106
Continental Engineering 83–4
cooperation 91-2, 144
corporate citizenship 74, 118–19,
    136
corporate responsibility 8, 74,
    136, 139–40, 173
    statements 73–5, 109
courage 31, 76–7, 88
credibility, organizational
    117–21
crisis, ability to deal with 39, 70
cultural diversity 138–42, 183–4
Cutler, Sandy 121

de Geus, Arie 100
death, Buddhist view of 95
decision maker
    competence of 3
    motivation of 3
    state of mind of 3
decision making 71
    and leadership 13–14
    applying Right View and
    Right Conduct to 15–16
    good 28
    importance of 8
    improving 40, 185
    process 18, 30
    quality of 30

decisions
  approaching from many
    perspectives 47
  communicating rationale for
    31
  effects of 18, 30
  fairness of 31
  making better 4
  making the right ones 3, 9,
    13–14, 17, 76–7, 185
  necessity of making 18
  quality of 3, 14
  success of 20
dependence on others 22
dependent origination 19–21,
  33, 69
  example of 20–21
Diener, Ed 107
dignity
  human 133
  lack of 70
discipline, ethical 36–7
diversity 9
  cultural 138–42, 183–4
downsizing 109
drives, self-oriented 2
Drucker, Peter 92

Eaton Corporation 121
economic system
  combining with moral values
    9, 185
  moral dimension of 180
economies
  free-market 4
  in socialist countries 4
economy
  responsible free-market 149,
    171–84
  sustainable 181–2
effort, enthusiastic 36, 38
Eight Worldly Concerns
  80–83
emptiness 23

Enron 31, 122
enthusiasm, 41
entrepreneurship
  Buddhist view of 149–50
  governments' role in
    stimulating 150, 155–63
  role in alleviating poverty
    149–70
environment
  concern for 75
  negative impacts on 2
environmental
  challenges 144–7
  responsibility 9
  sustainability 172, 181–2
  violations 117
equanimity 32, 43
Erasmus University 107
ethical
  dilemmas 112
  discipline 36–7
  standards 111–29, 144
ethics
  codes of 73
  in business 111–29
exploitative practices, in
  business 115–16

fairness 75
  lack of 70
faith
  building 71–2, 76
  combining with wisdom
    69–70
  inspiring 69, 92
  right kind of 69
family planning,Buddhist view
  of 161, 163
fanaticism, avoiding 45–6
Fay, Chris 126
flexibility 45–6
Fluor Corporation 120–21
focusing the mind 14
Forrester, Jay 15

free market
  and socialism 173–6
  positive aspects of 4
freedom 35, 37, 99, 151, 171–2, 185
  balancing with regulation 168–70
  Buddhist view of 169, 171–2
  democratic system based on 172
  limits to 169
  link with responsibility 179–81
  universal 181–84
free-market economies 4
Frey, Bruno 107
friendships, contribution to happiness 2

Gandhi, Mahatma 183–4
GE 72, 121–4, 128, 141
Gell-Mann, Murray 15
generosity 36
Gerstner, Lou 115
global economic system 18
global economy, concern for 1
global problems 1
globalization 185
  challenges of 133–48
good actions 29
Google 73
Goshn, Carlos 115
governance, corporate 111–29
governments
  collaboration with business 164–8
  role of 2
  role in stimulating entrepreneurship 150, 155–63
Grameen Bank 159
greed 36
Greenpeace 124–6

happiness 17, 73, 170, 171–2, 178–9, 184
  and business 102–10
  Buddhist concept of 2, 16, 110
  desire for 102
  government role in 2
  importance of 16
  research into 106–7
  role of friendships and relationships in 2
  role of wealth in 106–8
  root of 2
  what people are looking for 1
harm 32
  activities that cause 35
  avoiding 19, 30–31, 61, 137, 185
harmful products 116–17
Hayek, Friedrich von 179–80
Healthy Companies International 23
heart, warm and strong 89, 111, 129
heedfulness 34, 98
Herkströter, Cor 74, 125
Hirsch, Fred 106
His Holiness the Dalai Lama
  character of 34
  formal training 3–4
  leanings toward socialism 4, 173–4
  life of 5
  meetings with Mao Tse-Tung 174
  meetings with Nehru 154
  perspective on life 1
  relationships with other people 1
  responsibilities for Tibetan government-in-exile 1, 69, 171–2
  succession planning 89–90

view of communism 173–5
view of freedom 171–2
view of globalization 133–6
view of India 153–4
why he wrote this book 1
holistic approach 2, 4, 8, 15, 89,
    128, 136, 185
honesty 31
human rights 117, 123, 144, 151,
    171, 174, 182–3
humility 27, 31–2, 42, 89, 111, 128
Hut, Piet 64

IBM 115, 139–41
Immelt, Jeff 121–4, 128, 141
impermanence 14, 19, 22–4, 27,
    38, 62, 69, 89, 134, 137, 149
India
    environmental challenges in
        144–7
    fostering entrepreneurship in
        151–4
Indonesia 166–8
Indra, jewelry net of 22
inequality, 70, 170
ING 74
Ing, Nita 77, 83–4
injustice 70, 170
innovation 24, 40, 141, 166–8
insecurity about future 9, 70
integrity, role in leadership 8
intention 18–19
    right 14, 20
interaction of ideas 5
interconnectedness 1, 27, 33
interdependence 14, 19, 21–2,
    27, 69, 70, 133, 181–2, 184

job creation, government role in
    2
job satisfaction 102–10
    organizations' role in creat-
        ing 108–10
jobs, role of 103–4

karma, law of 29
Kerala 162
kindness 45, 61
knowledge transfer 110, 166–8

Land and Houses 59
Lay, Kenneth 31
Layard, Richard 107
leader
    behavior of 29
    character of 71, 76–9, 89,
        111
    demands on 79–80
    dependence on others 22
    developing 71
    purpose of 69–90
    selecting 71, 87–90
    state of mind of 19
    tasks of 71, 76
leadership 8, 18
    and decision making 13–14
    by example 33, 109
    continuity of 87–90
    holistic 9
    in a Buddhist way 76–7
    modest 36
    need to acknowledge
        universal responsibility 184
    understanding 3
    with a trained mind 79–84
living entity, organization as
    100–101

Mandela, Nelson 138–9
mantra, citing 64–5
Mao Tse-Tung, His Holiness the
    Dalai Lama meetings with
    174
Marsh McLennan 122
Marx, Karl 7, 178
Maslow, Abraham 103–5
Massachusetts Institute of
    Technology 14
meditation 39, 42–6

meditation
  analytical 32, 51, 60–62
  breathing 51
  effect on brain 51–4
  experiments with 52–3
  finding time for 49
  incorporating into daily life
    49
  mantra-citing 51
  one-pointed 33, 51, 59–60
  practicing 51, 54
  retreats 51, 54
  sitting 54, 58–9
  walking 51, 54, 55–6, 58
mental exercises 8
micro-credit 158–60
mind
  calm, clear and concentrated
    9, 14, 15, 19, 47, 71, 80, 185
  calming 62, 64
  improving 14
  training 5, 8, 9, 14, 15, 19, 20,
    30, 31, 33, 38, 39–41, 47–65,
    79–84, 105
mindfulness 15, 54, 55–6, 85–7
Minsky, Marvin 15
mistakes, ability to admit 31
mistrust of business 114–17
moral standards, influence of
  business on 101
moral values, combining with
  economic system 9
motivation 3, 14, 19, 81–82, 87,
  155
Myanmar 171
  human rights in 123

needs, hierarchy of 103–6
negative emotions 9, 14, 15,
  16–17, 25, 32, 37, 47–8, 59,
  62–3, 169
Nehru, Jawaharlal 154
net of Indra 22
Nike 127

Nissan 115
nongovernmental
  organizations, role of 126–8

Organization for Economic
  Cooperation and
  Development 119
organizations
  development of 135–6
  role in creating job
    satisfaction 108–10
Oswald, Andrew 107
Oxfam 166–8

Palmisano, Sam 139–41
past experiences, transferring to
  present 25–6
Patalung, Thitinart na, 26–7
patience 36, 37–8
Payutto, Venerable P. A. 93
peace 2, 5, 31
Perfections, Six 36–8
personal development 108–9
Philip Morris 117
philosophical questions 13
population growth, reducing
  rate of 2, 149, 161–3
population shifts 149
positional goods 106
poverty 9, 70, 103, 174
  alleviation of 1, 181
  Buddhist view of 99
  role of entrepreneurship in
    alleviating 149–70
principles, business 73
  characteristics of 74
  examples of Right Conduct
    75
principles, understanding 76
problems, Buddhist teachings
  on dealing with 80–83
process between cause and
  effect 20
profit 167–8

Buddhist view of 93–4, 110
   role in business 92, 93–4
Project Shakti 164–6
property rights 150, 156–7, 178
prosperity
   creating 186
   universal 181–84
purpose
   clarifying 76
   organizational 71–3, 91–2,
   102

reality, accepting 23, 25–6, 144
regulation, in relation to
   freedom 168–70
relationships with other people
   40, 101
   contribution to happiness 2
religious leaders, participation
   in global business 1
reputation 22, 87, 94, 111–29
respect 103, 109, 138
responsibility
   link with freedom 179–80
   universal 9, 133, 184
responsible free-market
   economy 149, 171–84, 185–6
Right Conduct 13, 15–16, 20,
   27–8, 35, 38, 65, 71, 74, 77,
   101, 111, 118, 124, 128, 144,
   145, 149, 169–70, 178, 185–6
   applying principles of 47
   benefits of 39–41
right livelihood 35–6, 116–17
Right View 13, 14, 15–16, 18–28,
   30, 31, 38, 65, 69, 71, 74, 77,
   83, 89, 101, 118, 124, 128, 137,
   144, 145, 149, 151, 162, 167,
   169–70, 178, 185–6
   applying principles of 47
   benefits of 39–41
   example of 85–6
Rosen, Robert H. 23
Rothermund, Heinz 124–6

Royal Dutch/Shell 74, 116,
   124–8

Santa Fe Institute 15
satisfaction surveys 108
satisfaction with life 1, 3
Satyanarayana, Masabathula
   146–7
scandals, business 36, 70, 111
secular ethics 2
seeing reality 20, 38, 69
self, Buddhist concept of 105
self-actualization 104
self-centeredness 16, 18
self-confidence 32, 33, 107
self-discipline 76
self-knowledge 78
Seligman, Martin 107
Senge, Peter 14–15, 100
shame 44–5
Singh, Manmohan 151–4
Smith, Adam 176–9
Smith, James 126
social responsibility 124
socialism, and free market
   173–6
socialist economies 4, 173–6
South Korea 153, 164
spiritual teacher, seeking 49–51
stakeholders, definition of 74–5
Stutzer, Alois 107
succession planning 87–90
suffering 32, 170
   alleviation of 3
   Buddha's view of 16
   desire to avoid 102
   existence of 3
sustainable development 9, 74,
   181–2
systems thinking 14

Tanti, Tulsi 144–6
Thailand, business leaders in
   39–41

thinking the right way 14
Tibet 171–2, 184
    cultural heritage of 171, 184
    demonstrations in 171–2
    establishment as
    autonomous region 89
    government-in-exile of 1, 69,
    89–90
    repression in 171–2
training the mind 5, 8, 9, 14, 15,
    19, 20, 30, 31, 33, 38, 47–65,
    105
    benefits of 39–41
    exercises for 48, 55–65
    for leadership 79–84
    purpose of 48
triple bottom line 74
trust 102–3, 109, 142
Tutu, Archbishop Desmond 161

unemployment 103
Unilever 164–8
United Nations 182, 184
    Declaration of Human
    Rights 102
    Global Compact 119
universal responsibility 133,
    147–8, 184
unwholesome
    actions 32–4
    consumption 106
    factors 41, 42–6

values
    defining 73–4, 76
    human 2
    need for in economic system
    185
    organizational 71, 73–5
Veenhoven, Ruut 107
vegetarianism, 35
view from many perspectives
    24
vigor 45

virtue, organizational pursuit of
    121–4
visualization exercises 62–4

wants, freeing yourself from 110
war 35, 70
wealth
    Buddhist concept of 2, 110
    check list for proper use of
    97–9
    creating 94–9
    desire for 43
    distribution of 178
    gaining legally 35
    generation of 178
    government role in creating
    2
    improper use of 94–5
    inequality in 186
    right use of 95–9
    role in happiness 106–8
Welch, Jack 72–3, 121
wellbeing of others, concern for
    32, 41, 42–4, 71, 75, 111, 148,
    183–4, 185
wholesome
    actions 32–4
    consumption 106
    factors 42–6
wisdom 36, 38
    combining with faith 69–70
    combining with generosity
    36
wishful thinking 25–6
work, Buddhist concept of 2
workforce diversity 123–4
Working Diamond, 26–7
World Bank 146–7, 157
World Database of Happiness
    107
worry 43–4

Yao, Kris, 40
Yunus, Muhammad 159

ACKNOWLEDGMENTS

This book is the result of teamwork and we would like to thank all those who participated.

In our meetings in Dharamsala, the two authors benefited from the constructive contributions of Tendzin Choegyal, the youngest brother of His Holiness the Dalai Lama; Tenzin Geyche Tethong, Private Secretary of His Holiness, former monk and minister in the Tibetan government-in-exile; and Ven. Lhakdor, a monk who is head of the Tibetan Library in Dharamsala.

Jan Kalff (former CEO of ABN Amro) and Folkert Schukken (former member of the Board of Management of SHV) in the Netherlands reviewed the many versions of all the chapters to make sure that the texts were helpful to business-people and contributed with their own very extensive experience. Cor Herkströter (former CEO of Shell and chairman of the board of ING) shared his experience of developing and implementing business principles in global organizations, especially in Royal Dutch/Shell. Sir Leonard Peach shared his experience from IBM and working with government.

Ven. P. A. Payutto from Thailand contributed with insights from Theravada Buddhism. Phra Ajahn Surasak Khamarangsi guided Laurens' retreat. Sirithorn Rutnin and Thitinart na Patalung organized additional practical guidance in the application of Buddhist principles.

Nicholas Brealey, our publisher, recognized the importance of the message in this book at an early stage. He played a vital role in structuring, sequencing and concentrating the message to make the text accessible and interesting for a wide public. Our editor Sally Lansdell made the text flow and ensured that the different sections fitted logically together.

Without my son Jörgen this project would not have begun. He raised my interest in Tibet and in His Holiness the Dalai Lama. My wife Maria-Pia has had to put up with a husband who, once he gets into a subject, can think and talk about nothing else, That meant that when the subject was Adam Smith, she got Adam Smith, for breakfast, lunch, dinner and as a nightcap, for several days until the next subject took over. To both my son and my wife, my thanks.